HANDMADE GREETING CARDS

for

SPECIAL OCCASIONS

HANDMADE GREETING CARDS

for

SPECIAL OCCASIONS

STEP-BY-STEP TECHNIQUES & 30 ORIGINAL
CREATIVE PROJECTS TO MAKE

AMANDA HANCOCKS

STERLING PUBLISHING CO., INC.
NEW YORK

TO KEVIN

Library of Congress Cataloging-in-Publication Data Available

10 9 8 7 6 5 4 3 2 1

Published by Sterling Publishing Co., Inc.
387 Park Avenue South, New York, NY 10016

© 2007 by Amanda Hancocks

Created by Lynn Bryan, The BookMaker, London
Photography and projects by Amanda Hancocks

Distributed in Canada by Sterling Publishing
C/o Canadian Manda Group, 165 Dufferin Street,
Toronto, Ontario, Canada M6K 3H6

Distributed in the United Kingdom by GMC Distribution
Services, Castle Place, 166 High Street, Lewes,
East Sussex BN7 1XU, England

Distributed in Australia by Capricorn Link (Australia) Pty. Ltd.
P.O. Box 704, Windsor, NSW 2756, Australia

Printed in China
All rights reserved

Sterling ISBN-13: 978-1-4027-4026-8
          ISBN-10: 1-4027-4026-3

For information about custom editions, special sales, premium
and corporate purchases, please contact Sterling Special Sales
Department at 800-805-5489 or specialsales@sterlingpub.com.

Opposite
Transparent paper, a cut-out stamp pattern, repeated, and sparkly tiny diamonds all combine in this greeting card.

Previous page
A collection of cards made by hand looks as good as a professional set!

Following page
You have mail! Your cards are on display.

CONTENTS

INTRODUCTION

I have been making greeting cards by hand since I was a child. Then, I would glimpse a piece of spare paper or card, a ruler, a pencil, and a scrap of fabric and instantly my mind would work out the design for a card for someone. Later, I became more adventurous, making stationery kits as gifts.

My chosen hobby then became a small business, quite by chance, through my other interest, which is photography. A friend and I were sorting through his portfolio and one of his images inspired me—a photograph of a calm Parisienne landscape.

I found some tracing paper and a piece of card, and mounted the image as a card. He liked it, as did other people, so I made other cards, adding relevant quotes, and took them to a local store. Happily, the owner ordered some stock and it sold out in a few weeks!

I took space at a trade show, with a range of forty-five cards, and was inundated with orders. Thus began my photography-based greeting card business. When I ran out of family album pictures, friends offered me theirs. Years later, my card designs have moved on, too, and feature far more than photographic images.

What I love about making cards by hand is the personal message they offer to someone important to you. The type of card you end up making depends on to whom you are sending it; the more special a person is to you, the more personal the design will be because you want there to be a surprise in store when the person opens the envelope.

Designing a card is a creative process that can be inspired by the smallest thing—a leaf, a color, a textured sheet of paper, or even a quote from a famous author or poet. The art is in being able to put all of the elements together in a cohesive design.

When I start the design of a personal card, I think about what the person means to me. I'll usually hunt through an old photo album to find a picture of the two of us that brings to mind that time we spent together. Hopefully, my friend will recall the same experience as the envelope is being opened.

For me, a card design can start with the paper, its color and its texture, then the remaining elements, shape and color, are decided. However, sometimes the shape of the card comes first. With other designs, the concept comes first, then the shape. As you can see, there are no hard and fast rules! However, one of my rules is that the back of the card must be as interesting as the front. Sometimes I wrap a design around the card.

I always look for the most fashionable colors because fashion has a big influence on everything. Interestingly enough, women's lace undergarments and other delicate items of clothing are a tremendous inspiration.

You will also see images of butterflies, dogs, cats, and fairies, and such decorative embellishments as stamped flower shapes, jewels, satin or velvet bows, lace, transparent paper, and little tags stamped with a person's name on my cards. The continual challenge is to combine that creativity with engineering shapes out of cards and textured papers—at the moment, I love to use parchment papers.

Several layers on a card are one of my design trademarks. Also, I've recently fallen in love with the concept of shiny hand-foiled cards, and you will definitely find one or two in the project section!

If you like the idea of using photographs of your family and friends, take a moment to look through old family albums, making a note of amusing, quirky, or interesting images for future reference.

In this book, I hope to provide you with the basic knowledge you need to begin the creative process involved in making a card. Once you have mastered the various artistic techniques, you will be able to develop your own recognizable style.

The approach I've taken is to simply show you that you can make a greeting card out of materials you might already have lying around the home. Scraps of fabric, pieces of card, and all-purpose glues can be put to use making cards, as can glitter, ribbons, buttons, and bows. Cans of fine spray adhesive make gluing fabric easy. Precut cards in many basic shapes are available if you have a lot of cards to make for an event.

All of the techniques are described in easy-to-follow language and are accompanied by step-by-step photography. In a few projects, you will see some of the how-to instructions are not accompanied by a photograph. This is because I felt the instructions were enough. (Too many images *can* be intimidating!) There are some instances where a knowledge of computer Word programs is useful, but do not worry if you do not have a clue about computers. You can write the words by hand. "Nothing too complicated" became my mantra during the making of this book!

Most of all, I want to share my passion for making cards. I hope the next greeting card you send is one you made yourself.

AMANDA HANCOCKS

Tools & Materials

TOOLS & EQUIPMENT

To make a greeting card by hand requires the right tools for a professional result. In this section you will discover the tools and learn how to make the materials magically transform your design.

The fun of making cards by hand begins with the selection of basic tools and accessories that assist you in making cards. You might find you already have most of them at home. A sharp pair of scissors for cutting paper and card is top of the list. A steel ruler is best for use with a craft knife. You can't cut into it as sometimes happens with a plastic ruler. A pair of pinking shears prevents fabric from fraying and is useful for giving a fancy edge to a piece of thick card.

Felt-tipped and embossing pens are useful in many ways. A dual embossing pen features one end that leaves a light glue when you paint over the outline on a stamp. When you add glitter or sequins to the stamped image on the card, the materials will stick to this glue.

A sharp pencil is essential for drawing templates, rubbing over lettering and generally making notes of measurements when you are at the early design stage.

Above

A bone folder to make creases in card and paper, a craft knife and ruler, a pink felt-tipped embossing pen, a blue Emboss Dual pen (double-tipped for outlining stamps with a sticky surface), gold and silver writing pens, a pencil, a pair of pinking shears, and a pair of paper-cutting scissors.

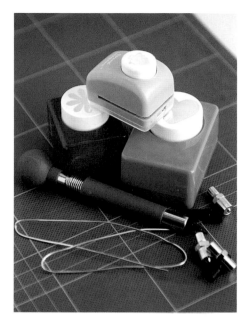

A cutting mat with a hole punch, three shapes of the many craft punch shapes available, and craft wire for making wire shapes.

A selection of glue materials: spray adhesive in a can, all-purpose glue, two types of glue stick, and glue tape.

A selection of glitter glues which are great for decorative touches on all cards, especially for children and young teenagers.

A selection of small plastic tubes of glitter that can be scattered over an area of card that has been made sticky with glue.

Paints for use on glass or transparent paper. The tall tube contains contour-lining paste for marking stained glass windows.

Two stamp designs, of hundreds available, that can be inked to make an impression on paper or card, with some silver embossing powder.

TYPES OF PAPER

The greeting card begins with the type of paper you select. A basic knowledge of paper weights and their unique qualities will help you make the right choice.

There are many different kinds of card and paper available as single sheets or in a roll (wallpaper is just one type in a roll). Getting the right paper for the task you want it to perform makes all the difference. If the paper or card is not right, then the card will not look as fabulous as it did in your mind when you designed it.

The first point to remember is that card and paper are referred to in terms of weight, thickness, and size. The weight is described in terms of "gsm," which means "grams per square meter." (Where used in the general projects, it is referred to as "g.") The weight you select is crucial to the success of your card design, especially if you are making a tall card and adding layers to it. It needs to be substantial enough to hold the "extras" and not fall over when the lucky recipient puts it on the mantelpiece.

I use any paper weighing more than 240gsm to make most of my cards.

Above left
Deep blue thicker tissue paper; a handmade paper with leaves; pale blue tissue paper; and a clear paper printed with dots.
Above right
Manufactured papers with interesting textures.
Left Papers in primary colors allow you to experiment with design.
Far left
Exquisite handmade papers from Japan are inspirational, and are more expensive.

Second, papers are either made by hand or manufactured by machine.

Manufactured papers feature fibers that run in the same direction. You can clearly see this if you hold a sheet of quality paper up to the light. In the trade, this is called the grain. Working with the grain, as opposed to against it, is important for success. My number one rule is to fold (crease) the paper in the direction of the grain. If you don't do this, then the fold will look less firm.

If you want to tear the edge of a card as part of the design, you will get a better rough edge if you go against the grain. This is the only time I would recommend going against the grain.

Some manufactured papers include fluted paper in a range of clear primary colors; metallic papers in copper, gold, and silver; pearlized papers in pale shades, plus the more traditional marbled finish. Papers are antiqued, made to look like fine crocodile and lizard skins, and even given a smooth matte stainless steel finish. I like to use translucent paper, which comes plain, printed with dots, or in a grid pattern. Also, clear acetate sheets (a combination of acetate and cellulose) are useful for creating an outer layer on a card. I have used some acetate in the projects.

Embossed papers with a pearlized coating, reminiscent of times gone by, are exquisite for use in wedding and anniversary cards.

Some manufacturers and paper importers provide a sample service, so contact one in your state and ask for a sample to experiment with before you start the project.

Handmade papers are available in a wide choice of designs. Some feature natural flowers and leaves, others show off flecks of metallic threads such as silver or gold. These are the papers that bring a card to life, especially if it is for a special occasion such as a wedding or an anniversary.

As handmade papers become more popular, individual paper manufacturers are producing some fabulous designs. Find the nearest paper store and spend some time looking though the selection of papers before starting the design process. The inspiration might come from the paper!

The size of the sheet or roll of paper is not a problem unless you are making a lot of cards at the same time. Most

Above

White embossed paper with a pearlized sheen is brilliant for wedding card designs.

square and standard-shaped cards can be cut from one regular-sized sheet of paper. Larger sheets of handmade paper are harder to cut so you must be accurate with the measurements to ensure you get as many as possible from the piece. When you buy it, ask the assistant to roll it so you don't end up with creases.

When you get home, unroll the paper and place it flat on the worktop, perhaps adding a heavy book or two to make sure it lies flat before working with it. Have fun creating!

SELECTING ENVELOPES

When you send a card, the envelope is the first thing the recipient sees when the card is delivered. The following pages reveal how to to make that first impression count.

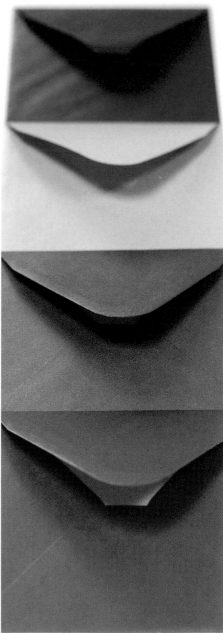

Let me say up front that I find any kind of envelope exciting. Envelopes are the harbinger of the style of the greeting card and, as such, ought to be as well "dressed up" as the card.

Texture is the first thing I look for in an envelope. What it feels like is important to the recipient and reflects the regard in which you hold this lucky person. I like to see a thick envelope with that smart, handmade look that sends a unique message. A contrast in the textures of the envelope and the card is a fine look, too. For a sophisticated look, use a cream thick envelope, with a smooth paper for the card to go inside.

Handmade papers make stylish envelopes; just make sure the address is legible on the paper. You can use a label but that might spoil the image. Also, remember the card has to go through the mail system and must be able to withstand the wear and tear it might encounter along the way.

Then I look for color. Does it match the colors I used in the card? Or can I get away with a sharp contrast such as a black envelope for a red card? Using the same color for the card and the envelope is also advised as long as the two colors match. There's nothing worse than two pinks that are not exactly the same hue.

The size of an envelope is integral to the card. Always measure the envelope you want to use before you begin to make the card. A small card placed in an envelope that is too big for it will not look right, not will a square card in a rectangular envelope.

Also think about how the envelope can be sealed. Even those with their own adhesive strips can be made more interesting with a wax seal, or a sticker or two. If you have your own initial seal, use this on warm wax to reinforce who is sending the card.

Stickers are fun envelope accessories for adults, too, for all occasions. When sending a card to a child, add a few stickers of a favorite cartoon character to the back of the envelope at the point where it seals.

Other decorative designs can be added to the envelope. If you have used the embossing technique as part of the card's design, then use it on the front of the envelope, too.

A final word. You can also wrap an envelope with ribbon or decorative string if you are presenting the card in person. This idea works well when you have a three-dimensional card which makes the envelope looks bulky when placed inside it.

Opposite left
Glorious gold and silver envelopes are printed with a seasonal greeting.

Opposite right
Here is just a selection of the many colors available in manufactured envelopes.

Above
Shades of beige and gray dominate in this collection of smooth envelopes and matching cards.

MAKING A SPECIAL-SIZED ENVELOPE

Making an envelope for a special size involves more than a few steps. However, the recipient will love the idea that you have made the envelope, too.

To start, you need a large piece of paper about twice the size of the folded card. Use a paper between 100g and 140g. A lighter paper can look insubstantial and heavier paper does not fold well.

Use glue tape because this will stick the edges immediately, and make sure you are firm when creasing and folding.

TIPS

• *Make sure the card fits inside the envelope at the start.*

• *All angles should be square to give the envelope a neat look.*

1

Cut a piece of envelope paper 1½" (40mm) wider on each side of the folded card and just under twice the width (for the flap that will be folded from the bottom), and 1½" (40mm) for the flap that will fold over from the top.

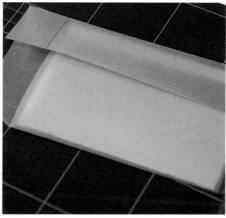

5

Using the top pencil line on the seam of the flap, draw a diagonal to form the flap angle.

The final envelope is the perfect size for this card.

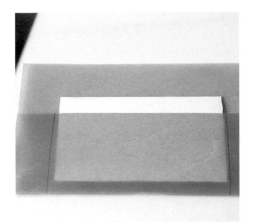

2

Lay the greeting card onto the paper that you are going to make the envelope out of and fold up the bottom flap so it is about three-quarters of the way up the card. Make a mark 1" (25mm) in from the edges on each side and draw a line down as above.

3

Open out the paper to make the envelope back. Cut along the drawn pencil lines and along the fold out to the edge. This will leave you with a flap. Then draw a line on the top flap about ⅛" (3mm) from the bottom flap.

4

Fold the flap up. Add the card, then cut diagonally from the bottom left and right of the two edge flaps. Fold the top flap over the bottom flap with the card still inside to get an idea of the bulk. Leave ¼" (6mm) border at the top and bottom. Draw a line on the top flap ⅛" (3mm) away from where the card rests on the top flap.

6

Using a knife, cut along the seam toward the top of the point of the flap. You are cutting out the flap shape.

7

Using the ruler to get a straight fold, line the ruler up along the edge of the card, allowing a ¼" (6mm) gap, then fold the two side flaps in. Then open the flaps out, ready for gluing.

8

Trim the small right-angle triangle off the top corners so it folds in easily. Then pull the bottom flap down. Fold the two side flaps into the center. Glue the bottom flap along both edges. Fold the flaps up and seal.

COPY AN EXISTING ENVELOPE

Here is a simple way to make a standard-sized envelope for a standard-size card. The weight of the envelope paper can match the weight of the card if you want to have a uniform look.

Above
Here, a bow, a small photograph, a cut-out paper flower, and a sequin star make all the difference to the back of the envelope.

This is quite an easy envelope to make. It is a matter of being very careful when outlining, in pencil, the shape of the existing envelope.

To me, the back of the card, where it is sealed, is the place for creativity. You can use commercial stickers (bought by the packet), or you can make a small bow and glue this to the top flap, add a small photograph of the recipient over

the point where the two flaps meet, or add small embellishments along the entire length of the seal.

The main thing is to remember too many embellishments might spoil your pretty envelope, so go easy on the number of items! You can use a stamp to cut out a shape of a flower and glue the flower in place, as I did.

Small touches count a lot.

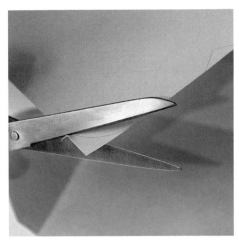

1

Peel the envelope apart carefully so you undo all the glue.

2

Lay the selected envelope out on the piece of paper you will use for the new envelope. Holding it firmly in place, draw around all of its shapes, making sure you pencil in all of the small shapes. Cut out the new shape carefully along the pencil line.

3

Use sharp paper-cutting scissors to cut the small lines (above and Step 4). Use a steel ruler and a knife to cut the straight lines.

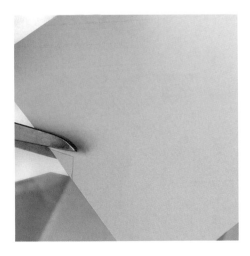

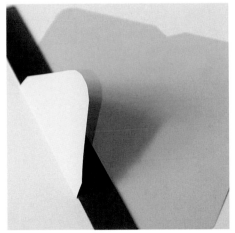

4

Use the tips of the scissor blades for a fine and precise cut.

5

Using a ruler, firmly fold the new card shape along the straight lines. Fold the two side flaps in.

6

Using glue tape, glue along the outer edges of the bottom flap. Press the bottom flap down onto the two folded side flaps. Then place the card in and seal with the same glue.

READY-MADE CARD SHAPES

If you are going to send more than 10 cards, buying ready-made blank cards and adding decorative embellishments to them is the easier option.

Blank cards come in many shapes and sizes and are usually made to go with an envelope of the same size. The common shapes are square, rectangular, and thin and vertical. These blank cards are generally made of quality paper.

A good range of colors is available and you can select plain blanks, or blanks with oval, square, or rectangular cutouts. You can add a photograph or a clear cellophane bag filled with stars or sequins *(see page 30)*.

The big question is, Which shape for which type of card? The answer depends on the design you're planning.

Anything tall and slender requires a thinner, vertical shape, and something square or round requires a square card.

I've found there are two ways to work. You can select the card shape first, then see, by placing the items around the card, how the decorative motifs will work on the shape. The other way is directly the opposite. You might have a collection of materials you want to use, so you have to work out the design on a sheet of paper, then select a card shape to suit your design.

For example, a seaside theme might look best on a dark cream-colored card which has a thick, rough texture. The shape ought to be horizontal, reflecting a long stretch of beach. Any shells ought to be in proportion to each other and to the size of the card.

Analyze the cards you like and take notes on the basic design rules.

MAKE A SINGLE-FOLD CARD

A simple single-fold card is the basic card type for many of the projects you will make as you learn your craft. Here's how to make a 5" (125mm) square shape from a regular sheet of paper.

1 _____

Take a single sheet of paper and fold it in half, lining up the edges to give you a straight line along the fold.

2 _____

Measure 5" (125mm) down from the top edge and make a pencil mark and then cut through both layers.

Have your tools ready, including a cutting mat, a steel ruler, a sharp craft knife, a pencil, and a bone folder.

My number one rule is to fold the paper in the direction of the grain, so make sure you follow this example.

Creasing the fold with a bone folder will give it an extra-sharp crease, too. You can also turn the paper inside out and crease it along the inside of the fold for an even sharper fold. Then fold the card back to the right side.

Try not to make the crease too sharp because this action might tear the paper. It depends on the thickness of the paper. You want the fold to be sharp but not too sharp.

If you are concerned the finished card does not look square, check it with a set square.

3 _____

Then measure 5" (125mm) from the crease to the pencil mark. Cut out the square firmly, using the craft knife.

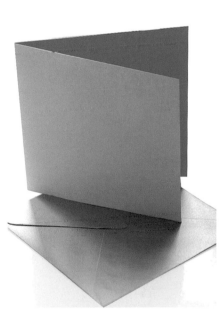

Opposite

A selection of precut card blanks includes cards with cutouts, some brightly colored square shapes, and cards with rough edges.

MAKE A THREE-PANEL CARD

The three-fold card can be made with an aperture on the front panel, or left simply as a concertina card.

1

To begin, cut a piece of paper or card in a size that can be divided into three. The card shown on the cutting mat measures 10½" (270mm) along its longest side.

If your piece of paper is larger and needs to be cut to size, mark off the top and bottom to measure 10½" (270mm) and trim off, leaving the height as is. (The height of the card is not so relevant and you can make it as tall as you think it can stand.)

Now measure 3½" (90mm) along the long edge at the top and bottom, then make a mark at 7" (180mm) at the top and bottom.

With the bone folder, make a mark along the 3½" (90mm) and 7" (180mm) marks, making a firm indent from top to bottom.

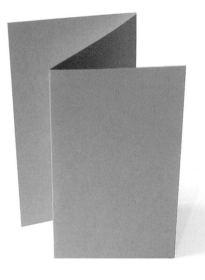

2

For the finalstep in making a three-fold card, cut a strip ⅛" (3mm) from the outside edge of the right-hand panel. The panel folds in to cover the back of the middle panel.

3

For a concertina card, make the first mark on one side of the paper, and the second on the other side. Fold the front in toward the middle panel, and the back to the middle.

CUT AN APERTURE

Apertures are an excellent way of displaying personal photographs, a piece of fabric, a clear cellophane window, or any other decorative element that needs a frame.

1

On the front of the card, measure an equal space in from the top, side, and lower edges. Make small pencil marks on the card along the ruler's edge. Join up the lines with pencil, making a frame in the shape you want. Use a light pencil because you'll need to erase them if any are left showing.

2

Cut along all of the lines with a craft knife and a steel ruler. Do this carefully. If one corner does not cut as cleanly as the others, do not pull on the paper. Put the ruler back in place and use the tip of the blade to cut firmly where it is joined. It will work and the corner will look neat.

An aperture can be cut into the front of any card and can be of any size. Remember, though, that the size of the aperture ought to remain in proportion to the size of the entire card.

The aperture acts as a frame. You can stick a decorated panel onto the back of the frame, with the design showing in the frame, and also add decorative items to the front of the finished frame.

Almost anything can be used in the frame, for example a small piece of lace, a photograph, embroidery.

Apertures are also good to frame a phrase written on an insert. To do this, measure the area of the aperture onto the internal sheet exactly and make sure the words fit into the available space. Then you have created a window onto the world of words.

Reserve the aperture you've cut out because it can always be used in future projects to mount something on. Or you can use it to practice cutting out other shapes. You will be surprised at how many uses it has.

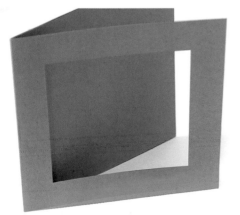

Left
The final card with is aperture ready to display the chosen work of art.

USE A TEMPLATE

There are ways to make apertures easier. One of them is to use a plastic template (as below) or a template you have made using thick card.

Shown (right) is a template with a number of shapes cut into it. The grid lines are there to help you align the template vertically or horizontally on the card. Lay the card out flat and check you are cutting through one layer only. To help you when cutting, make a series of light pencil marks at strategic places within the circle. Erase them afterward. It is not easy for a beginner unless you have a steady hand.

1

Draw around the inside of the required shape and cut it out with a sharp craft knife. Do this slowly and concentrate.

2

The final aperture and the piece that was cut out from it. Keep this piece for future use.

ADD A TRANSPARENT WINDOW

Adding a transparent acetate sheet to an aperture offers an array of decorative opportunities. It's easy to do, too.

1

Measure the size of the aperture to be covered. Write down the measurements, then add 1" (25mm) all around. This gives you enough space to stick the transparent sheet to the back of the aperture's frame.

Using a steel ruler to keep the lines straight, mark the measurements onto the acetate sheet. Then cut out the window using a sharp craft knife, keeping the ruler in place as a guide.

NOTE: If you struggle to cut all the way through a thicker transparent sheet, score it a few times firmly, then take it in your hands and flex it. The sheet will break cleanly along the scored lines.

2

Using glue tape, glue each edge of the frame on the inside of the card.

3

Take the transparent sheet and carefully put it in position over the streaks of glue tape. Press down firmly on all sides.

ALTERNATIVE IDEA

When making a window to put decorative things in, cut two pieces of the acetate exactly the same size. Glue one to the front of the card, over the aperture, then lay it out flat. Add the dried flowers, stars, glitter, or Happy Birthday words to the sheet, then glue tape along each side of the second sheet. Carefully lay the second sheet over the first and seal by pressing firmly. You will then have an enclosed panel.

ADD A TRANSPARENT POCKET

When you want to make an impressive card, try adding a small cellophane pocket filled with glitter and stars to the aperture.

This success of this technique lies in the size of the aperture and the cellophane pocket. (These are easily available from craft websites and stores.) The key is to make the aperture slightly smaller than the size of the cellophane bag. It is easier to do it this way than to cut the aperture in the card then look for a cellophane bag to fit over it.

You can tip anything you like in the bag, including gold or silver Happy Birthday words, confetti, glitter, and small dried flowers.

Try to use light-weight decorative things so the bag doesn't lean the front of the card over when you stand it on the shelf.

Let your imagination loose and see what designs you can make.

Left

The final card is a pretty picture in pink with razzle-dazzle glitter with flower shapes scattered through it.

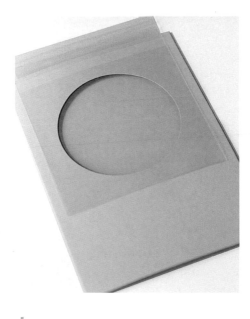

1

Place the cellophane bag, with the opening at the top, over the aperture to ensure it fits.

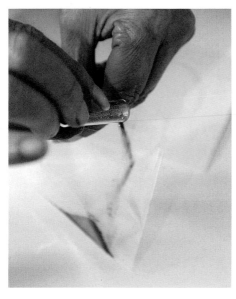

2

Take the bag in hand and fill it with pink glitter and some punched pink flowers.

TIPS

• *Select a thin cellophane bag so you can see through it clearly.*

• *Use a tiny spoon to add the glitter or small beads. This will control the flow better.*

• *When you seal the bag, shake it up and down to check it is sealed tightly and that nothing is going to escape.*

• *When gluing the bag to the inside of the front of the card, place the lower edge as close to the bottom of the aperture as possible. Doing it this way will ensure everything in the bag can be seen from the front.*

• *Don't glue this lower edge because it sits so close to the aperture and glue might show through.*

3

Seal the bag well with sticky tape, making sure the tape will not show in the aperture.

4

Using all-purpose glue along the top edge and both sides, stick the bag to the card.

ADD AN INSERT

This is one of my favorite looks for a card. This technique is all about layering and decorating to make an impression on the lucky recipient.

An insert is an easy thing to make yet it adds a wonderful visual appeal to any type of card.

Make the insert slightly smaller than the exterior translucent card. If you aim to print a message on the insert, do this before attaching the insert to the card. You might also want to add a personal handwritten message before you glue. It is just easier to do it that way.

The outer layer has a frosted look and is enlivened by the flower shapes on the front, which were stamped before adding the insert. The flowers have a dual purpose because they let the color shine through. Use a stronger color because paler colors might not show through as well through this thicker translucent card.

Right
Layering a frosted translucent outer layer over a colored insert lends an elegance to this card.

1

Cut the translucent card to the final shape required. The folded front measures 5" x 5" (125mm x 125mm). Then fold the insert paper in half and cut the insert to measure ⅛" (2mm) smaller on all four sides, which is 4¾" (120mm) square.

2

Run a line of glue tape on the spine of the back side of the insert.

3

Open out the translucent card so you can clearly see the spine. Holding the insert in both hands, align the back of the insert with the glue on it to the back of the translucent card. Press it firmly into place.

4

The insert is now glued to the back of the translucent card. The card is ready to decorate.

TIPS

• *The weight of the insert paper should be lighter than the translucent outer layer.*

• *Use a bone creaser to make sure you get a firm crease on both the translucent paper and the insert paper.*

33

EMBELLISHMENTS

Any scrap of material, a beautiful button, a length of ribbon, a packet of stars, or a tube of sequins can add star quality to a handmade card. Be visually inspired by ideas in this section.

Fabric

Large or small scraps can be used to create a signature style for your cards. The weight of a piece of fabric is not all that important. Felt, cotton, satin, wool (great for making little sheep!), tulle (netting), polyester, lace, linen, velvet, chiffon, and gingham are just a few of the types of fabric you can use.

The texture is important. If you want to make a card for a man or boy and want to add fabric (perhaps you are recreating his favorite suit or T-shirt) then a thicker fabric is preferable.

For a young girl or a woman, a feminine texture, such as velvet, lace, or satin, is an ideal addition to a card.

The texture and color of the fabric each depend on the style you want for the final card. For a party invitation, you need a hint of frivolity, so lace or satin are the perfect choice. You can also choose one smaller area of the fabric's design to place on the card—you do not have to use the entire piece.

For instance, you could make a paper template in the shape of a large dalmation dog and use it to cut out a piece of the spotted fabric for the dog's body. Add the fabric to a piece of card and you have the idea!

For a small boy, a scrap of material with a camouflage pattern can become a soldier's uniform on a plain green card.

A light fabric such as tulle is useful for bridal- and ballet-themed cards

because you can scrunch it up into a veil or ballet skirt or thread it with fine ribbon to make a ruched effect.

If you are using fabric to cover the front and back of a card, then it is best to spray the back of the fabric with adhesive then smooth it carefully onto the card.

Cutting Out a Shape

Sharp scissors are necessary to get an even edge. If the fabric is extra fine, use pinking shears when you cut it because they will give the fabric a diamond edge and prevent it from fraying.

If you find a piece of fabric with an embroidered pattern you could cut around the embroidered emblem and use it in a different way on a card. For instance, in the gingham (top left) there are several embroidered flowers. You could cut out a few and place them inside the card, or on the back of the card as an extra touch.

Felt is good for cutting out shapes of handbags, shoes, dogs, cats, houses, and vases. It is a strong fabric that does not lose its shape. Use an all-purpose glue rather than a spray adhesive for felt.

Draw a template of the desired shape, using a piece of of thin card or paper. Cut it out carefully then place on top of the piece of fabric. When you have finished with the template, do not throw it away. Keep all of the templates you make in a suitable box for the next card-making session.

Ribbons

When you think of ribbons you tend to think of bows alone but you can use ribbon in lots of ways. Thin ribbon is best for making bows for cards because it is more easily pulled into shape and is more in proportion to the size of the average card. That said, a large card will require a thicker ribbon!

On the wedding card in the project section I have used a wide, white velvet ribbon along the edge. It adds to the romantic look and is soft to the touch, giving the card a luxurious feel. Satin ribbon would not have looked right, nor would silk. I wanted something substantial and velvet was perfect.

Do consider the look and feel of a ribbon before adding it into your design. Think, too, about its color and pattern. A plain card can handle a patterned ribbon, but a patterned ribbon might clash with a patterned card, so perhaps use a single-color length of ribbon, either in a contrasting color or in a tone complementary to the card.

When using ribbon to hold several layers of card, paper, and parchment together, I like to use a thin, double-sided ribbon because then it looks the same on both sides. I also like to use a ribbon along the spine for an added touch of glamour and because it can often hold a design together and define the card.

Above

Ribbons can be textured and printed with a pattern or plain and textured, such as the thin velvet ribbon (top right). Ribbon cord is great for invitations or a congratulations card with an insert. Gold and silver are favorite colors for cords, but many colors are available.

Feathers

Fluffy and light in weight, feathers are perfect for instantly communicating fun and frivolity. Synthetic types are now available in all colors and shapes, which offers you a lot of design choices.

A small dab of glue on the tip of a feather is sufficient to keep it in place on a card. Too much glue can stick all of the fluffy bit down, which you don't really want to happen.

Real feathers would be fantastic on a card design for a young naturalist. You could gather three or four together and glue them to the bottom edge and use photographs of small birds' eggs as the main image, placed above the line of fine feathers.

Diamantés

Add a diamanté to any special occasion card, especially if it is in honor of Valentine's Day, or a loved one's birthday. Heart-shaped, round, or small rectangular diamantés convey the message quickly in a multitude of colors. Go for glamour all the way!

Easily glued onto ribbon or to the card itself, you can use them singly, in a line at the top or bottom, or in a small cluster. Consider colors in the same hues, and sizes that are in proportion to the size of the card.

Make sure you leave the card to dry before placing in the envelope. You don't want any of the diamantés falling off en route to your friend.

Glitter

Glittering designs are possible when you use star shapes, beads, and sequins.

Beads, too, are beautiful decorations and come in all shapes and sizes, and in a wide variety of finishes ranging from pearl to glass. You can buy flower beads, butterfly beads, pink heart beads, acrylic faceted beads, and tiny caviar beads.

Beads come in circular, ellipsed, and dewdrop shapes,

When attaching beads to your design, you might need a dab more glue than usual to make sure they stick to the card well. You might like to try glue dots or sticky pads. A bead with a flat back will stick more easily than a fully round bead. Do not use small beads on cards for small children in case they put the beads in their mouth.

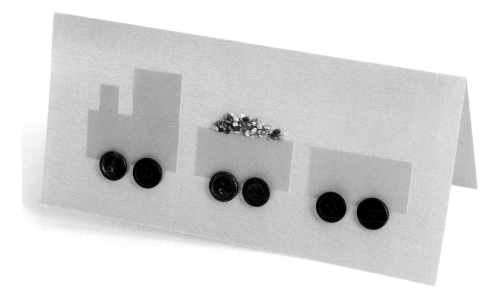

Buttons

Buttons are useful as decorative items for cards. Add a button to a card and it takes on a new personality. It can be a wheel on a small car or on a pram as in our project on page 102, a button on a snowman's coat, an earring on a girl's head, or an evening star in a galaxy.

You can use buttons as a border around a photograph, or as a wide border around the entire front of the card. If the recipient collects buttons, then using lovely buttons on a card creates the perfect design.

Flat-backed buttons (usually those with small holes for thread) are best because they can easily be glued to the card and will sit flat.

To buy interesting bottons, you can either go to a store known for its selection, or you can search for unique styles and colors at bring-and-buy markets and, if you have access to the Internet, there are many online sites that sell new and old buttons.

Also, your mother or grandmother might have an old sewing kit hidden away that you could look through to find some old buttons.

The usual design rules apply when using buttons. First, the size of the button ought to be in proportion to the size of the card and the place where it will be used.

Second, the color of the button ought to be in harmony with the color of the card, but the buttons need not necessarily be all the same color, especially if you are creating a clown.

Flowers

Fresh flowers are the ultimate for a card but it is, sadly, only possible to use them when you are going to hand the card to the person on the same day. Any cut flower wilts quickly.

However, dried flowers more than compensate for the lack of freshness. There are skeleton leaves, mini roses, rosebuds, blue delphiniums, lilies, sunflowers, daisies, and many more available through reputable dried flower companies online, or at craft stores.

The choice of flower will depend on the style of the card and the message you want to send. Roses are always the symbol of love. For the meaning of other flowers, do some research before deciding on which flower to use and avoid sending the wrong message.

Lettering

Rub-down lettering is a quick and easy way to write a word or phrase on the front of a card. Without this style of lettering, we would have to learn how to write in a more artistic way!

Fortunately, rub-down lettering comes in a choice of type styles and colors. Fun lettering, somber lettering, words and phrases in capital letters and in italic and ornate type styles.

Keep the sheets of lettering in a cool, dry place so they don't dry out. Seal the packet when you have used the lettering to protect the remaining sheets.

Use an orange stick or a pencil that has worn down to transfer the lettering to the card. See the Techniques section for more advice.

Stickers

Stickers are available in many different shapes and sizes and are great for using on theme cards. Does your friend like dogs? Use your imagination with stickers to create a family of dogs, or a group of dogs of the same breed on the front of the card.

Do you have a niece with a passion for fairies or ballerinas? There's sure to be a sheet of stickers waiting for you.

The other good place for stickers is on the front and back of envelopes. It is best to work out your placement before actually sticking one on the envelope or card, because if you make a mistake and want to remove it, the paper or card might tear.

Photocorners

To create a card with an old-fashioned style using a sepia-toned photograph you can use either a traditional clear mount or a natural paper mount to match the look of the photograph.

Roses, ladybugs, blue daisies, silver snowflakes, dragonflies, and even soccer balls are now appearing on self-adhesive photo corners.

Natural brown gift tags are also a useful design tool. They can hang from, or be glued to, a card and are great for writing personal messages on with a colored ink pen. They're not as dear as a shiny, coated gift tag but they can look just as good.

Wallpaper

You might think that using wallaper for a greeting card is a little out of the ordinary. However, wallpaper offers you a ready-made pattern on a paper with a good thickness. It is easily glued to a piece of card.

I like to use wallpaper as an overall cover for the front and back of a card, whether it is vertical or horizontal in shape. This is in line with my design philosophy of layering papers one on top of the other. Once you have decided on the card shape, add a layer of wallpaper on the exterior, then add a layer of thinner plain writing paper on the inside for your message. Tie all of the layers together with a thin ribbon wrapped around the spine.

The range of available wallpaper is fantastic. Many stores offer a cutting service that lets you cut a small strip to take home. One good thing about wallpaper is that rolls of it are often on special in DIY stores and this makes it attractive to use when you have to make a lot of cards.

Wallpaper designs range from small to large floral patterns and wide or thin stripes through to papers with a flock or a metallic finish. Some of the modern papers are like exotic works of art, with fleurs-de-lis, swirls, and squares in silver on black or red background, while the more traditional designs will make a good basis for a card for an older friend or family member.

Some patterns have a natural look, imitating linen or another such natural weave. These can look fabulous on a card for someone who is eco-minded.

You could add dried leaves or flowers, too, to carry on the natural theme. Patterns designed for children's rooms will make fun cards for a birthday boy or girl.

You can add embellishments such as gems, diamentes, and sequins to lengths of ribbon and hang the ribbon from the spine to make the card extra special.

Use spray adhesive on the back of the wallpaper (in a cardboard box) and smooth it over the flattened base card.

Photographs

Using a photograph on a greeting card presents a message in a personal manner. For inspiration, begin with the family album. Hunt it down and look through it with an eye to finding the right image for the message you want to send.

You might be surprised at the varied collection of iconic images of mother, father, sister, brother, grandmother, as well as family friends. You might even see them in a new light!

Every picture tells a story. These images will either make you laugh, resulting in a humorous card, or show the person in a serious light, resulting in a more subdued card design. It's the essence of the story you want to get across. The shape of the image might also determine the shape of the card. With luck, a quote suitable for the mood of the photograph will spring to mind. A book of quotes is a good investment if you plan to make more than a few cards.

A pair of "croppers" is also handy. These can be made from two thin lengths of card taped in an L-shape. You place the L-shape over sections of a photograph to help decide which part is the best to use for your design.

There are many other ways to use a photograph as an embellishment. For example, you can mount it on a card or foil frame and then place it on the front of the actual card so it can be removed later; place it in a shaped aperture; use several at a time; and perhaps place one within a border of ribbon or flowers.

Color photographs can look as interesting as older pictures, so think beyond the traditional sepia-toned and have fun with color, too.

A word of advice. Be kind. Avoid using a photograph showing someone in an embarrassing situation. You might think it's funny, but they might not.

In the following chapter I reveal how to reproduce favorite pictures so you can retain the original in perfect condition. I will also explain how to tint and how to age a black and white photograph by hand.

Techniques

USING ADHESIVES

Thanks to modern adhesives you can stick just about anything to anything else. Here is an introduction to my favorite types of glue.

There are several types of adhesive used in making craft projects. For example, the adhesive used for card and paper is different from the one you use for gluing dried flowers, sequins, or beads.

On these two pages you will find information on which adhesives are best for particular applications. Not shown, but also useful, are a simple paper adhesive that comes in a tube; glue dots, which are made on a long roll and come in a packet; double-sided tape; and fabric adhesive, which is either water-based or latex-based. Water-based is the best type for making cards because it is a white adhesive that dries clear and will not discolor over time.

Spray adhesive

The trick to successful spraying is to spray the item that is going to be stuck to the card.

For health reasons, and to avoid the spray sticking to a wider area, place the item to be sprayed inside a cardboard box adapted for this purpose. Open a window and spray down into the box. Spray in a smooth movement across the item to get an even coverage.

Spray mount is best for large pieces of fabric and paper.

Glue tape

This type of adhesive comes in a small plastic container that can easily be held in your hands. The glue comes out in a strip and is best for use along the edges of card and paper, particularly when creating layers on the front of a card, or when placing photographs or a thin acetate bag behind an aperture. It is also used to glue ribbon to the spine or other area of a card design.

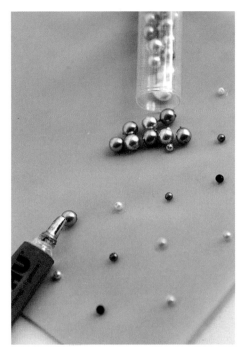

All-purpose glue

Here's a liquid glue that lives up to its name. Clear and fluid, it is best for use on small items such as beads, sequins, and diamantés in situations where other glues can't go. It is sticky, so press the tube gently each time you use it so the liquid comes out slowly. Always press near the bottom of the tube.

Sticky mounting pads

These are available in packs in a variety of sizes and thicknesses. Made of foam, they are used to raise a decorative item from the card it is being stuck to. They feature a small, peel-off strip on both sides of the pad. You peel one off and stick it to the item, then peel the other off (see right) before attaching it to the card. These are an indispensible tool when making cards.

USING BEADS & FEATHERS

Adding a beaded ribbon to the spine of a card can often be the finishing touch to a design. It is easy to do when you follow the instructions below.

First, decide on the combination of colors of the beads or feathers you want to use, as well as the combination of shapes and sizes. For the beaded ribbon effect shown below, I selected beads in both round and oval shapes.

Find the larger end bead first and work up from that point, selecting each of the smaller beads next, moving them around on the card until you are happy with the way the combination works. Then select the top bead.

> **TIP**
>
> • *Add a dab of pva clear-drying glue to the tip of the ribbon to seal it, and stop the ribbon from fraying on the back of the card.*

1

Lay the beads on the card in the order you want them to be used. Thread a needle with double thread ready to run through the holes in the middle of the beads.

2

Tie a big thick knot on the large end bead with the double thread to secure the bead. Thread through the first bead then back through to secure it, then thread all the beads together. Cut a length of thin ribbon (in a similar hue) just a bit longer than the height of the card.

3

Attach the string of beads to the ribbon with thread, not too close to the top because you do not want the ribbon to fray. Glue the ribbon onto the spine of the card, up and over the top at the spine, adding an extra dab of glue at the back the card. Trim the thread on the bottom of the bead. Let it dry for 20 minutes.

1

Select a variety of feathers and beads to use on the front of the card. Overlay the feathers in a random pattern.

2

Using an all-purpose adhesive, stick them to the card according to your design.

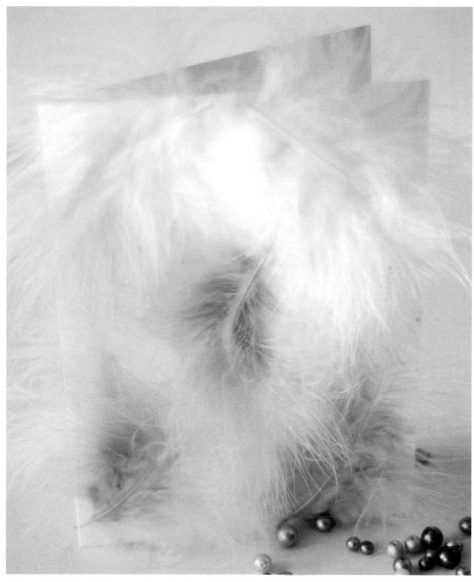

3

Don't worry about feathers overlapping the edges of the card, this just adds to the "floaty" feel. You are now ready to add other embellishments suchs the beads. Glue them to the feather's spine for security. I've used beads of different sizes and colors for variety.

Malibu feathers, which you can buy in packets, are perfect to create a romantic, soft the background. They make everything look lovely and glamorous.

Work carefully with these delicate decorations, using tweezers if you want. Once the card is covered in feathers, continue to layer the front of the card with embellishments such as diamentes, beads, and small satin ribbon bows.

EMBOSSING ON FOIL

Foil is a fabulous material to work with when designing a card. When it is embossed, it becomes an even more desirable decorative touch.

Embossing is the raising of a surface pattern on paper or on card. You can use the same process on tin foil. Here are the instructions on how to do it, using a christmas tree template.

First, cut a piece of foil to the size you desire for your tree shape. Then cut a piece of paper the same size. Follow the steps to make my foil christmas tree.

If the foil is slightly bent out of shape, you can flatten it by smoothing the foil afterward to make the branches flat. You can then adorn your foil tree with tinsel and diamante beads.

**EMBOSSING ON CARD
AND PAPER**

• *Use blotting or watercolor paper to create a lasting impression. Stamp out the shape. Then place a 100g sheet of paper over the stamped shape. Using the end of an empty pen, or an embossing tool, rub the outline (the edges) of the shape. Hold the paper firmly in position. Turn the paper over for the final result. Be firm but gentle because you don't want to tear the paper.*

1

With a pencil, draw an outline of a tree, as above, then cut it out using scissors. This is the template for the tree design.

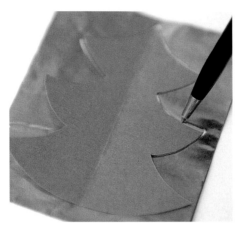

2

Hold the template in place on the foil temporarily with a glue dot. Using the tip of an old ballpoint, draw around the tree. Remove the template. Cut out the foil tree.

3

Draw circles and lines of tinsel on the back. Turn the foil over to see the embossed effect.

4

Add a dab of PVA glue and one ¼" (6mm) diameter flat-backed crystal to each circle.

TIPS

• *If you punch a hole in the top of the tree just down from the top, the recipient can take carefully remove the tree from the front of the card, tie a thin cord through the hole and then hang it on a live christmas tree.*

• *Make sure the image is not too large for the sheet of foil. Art and craft supply stores sell craft tin foil by the roll, which is a good investment if you are going to use foil in many of your designs. The material is easy to handle and you just keep it rolled up in the plastic bag you bought it in.*

5 _____

Add a purple star (this is a glittery star from a packet of confetti) to the top of the foil tree. Then add the entire design to the front of the card, using a sticky pad at the top and one on each side of the lower edge.

DESIGN WITH INK

Using water and ink to paint a pattern on a sheet of thick paper or card is a timeless technique called colorwashing.

The reaction between water and a colored ink produces a unique and enchanting result on a sheet of wet paper. Once the drop of ink touches the wet paper you have no control over what effect it will produce. When you add the effect of a tiny amount of bleach as well, you get some interesting patterns.

You can use this effect on large sheets of paper (to act as a gift wrap to match a card), or use it on smaller pieces as a panel on the front of a cards, or on a separate bookmark which you can attach to a card.

Before you start, protect the work surface with a piece of waterproof material such as plastic sheeting.

On the opposite page is a photograph of one of the projects in the chapter later in the book. It shows how I have used a piece of inked and bleached paper on the front of a card.

TIPS

• *Avoid over-wetting the paper.*

• *If your card crinkles up when it is dry, place the sheet of paper within two clean sheets of white paper and then place the sheets under a pile of heavy books overnight.*

1

Wet a sheet of thick white card by running it under a faucet. Place the card on a protected surface and drip blue ink into the wet card.

2

Using a damp paintbrush spread the ink over the surface of the entire sheet.

3

To bleach this paper, pour a small amount of bleach into the the container cap. With a brush, dab bleach onto the wet surface.

4

Work carefully over the whole surface. If the card starts to dry too quickly add more plain water. Don't add more bleach. Leave to dry.

USING PHOTOGRAPHS

Pictures from the past bring back memories of moments you enjoyed with family and friends. Share these images with those people to being a smile to their faces.

By this stage you will have found the family album and decided which of the photographs to use. How do you reproduce the original?

There are two ways to do this. Readers who own a computer and a scanner will already be aware of the process. Place the image(s) on the scanner and scan at 300 dots per inch (dpi). This results in an excellent quality image which can be saved as a "tiff" (an image file name.) Using Photoshop, work out the size at 100 percent. The image is now ready to print.

If you are using a digital camera, download the images to your computer, then edit and size them in the program of your choice. Save them as a tiff at a high resolution (300 dpi) and print out onto photo paper.

If you do not have a computer or a scanner, then the photocopier is your friend. Place the image on the glass, and copy it at 100 percent on quality paper. If you want to make it smaller or larger use the machine's settings. You can also copy several at a time to print on a letter-sized sheet of photo paper. Cut out each image when you need it.

Copy sepia-toned images in color to retain the effect. Trim each photograph.

Editing the images is important to get rid of extraneous elbows, half a head, a thumbs-up, or whatever else is in the frame but not relevant. Also, focus on the people and their body language. That's where the humor is hidden!

Aging & color-tinting a photocopied photograph

1

Select the image and copy it onto slightly thicker paper. Pour water into a saucer and place a used tea bag to one side.

2

Lightly dip the tea bag into the cold water, squeeze it until just damp, then rub it over the surface in one smooth movement.

3

The final image. When dry, place the image under a heavy book to flatten it ready for use on the card.

4

You can also create a sepia-effect using half a sachet of instant coffee mixed in cold water. Using an artist's paintbrush and making broad strokes allows you to control the density of the sepia more easily.

Color-tinting

Work on a copy of the original, on thicker paper. Take a blank page from an album as a background. Using a fine brush and a palette of watercolors, tint areas of the picture one at a time. Do this in a light area of the room so you can see precisely what you are doing.

2

Rinse the brush between colors to retain each hue. The brush must not be too wet. Use light strokes and work slowly building up the color. Try to achieve a subtle wash rather than a blob of color. You want to be able to see the image through the color.

USING NATURAL MATERIALS

Nature provides cardmakers with a wonderful array of leaves and flowers to use as decoration on the front of cards or as the base for an overall design.

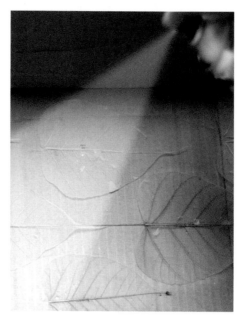

1

Select the size and color of the leaves you want to use and lay them in groups on the background card. This example uses four different leaves.

2

Layer the leaf or leaves, wrong side up, in the bottom of an old cardboard box and spray back and forth in one smooth movement. Spray the leaves in batches just before you work with them on the card.

3

Place the leaves overlaying each other so you cover the entire card. Here you can see there is a pattern emerging with the large, fine leaves as the first layer.

Natural plant leaves and dried flowers are available in packets either from online craft websites or from a local craft store. If you live in the country, or near a park, then Nature will provide. Make sure you wash and dry natural leaves before use.

Leaves can be used individually, in a pattern on card, or used in layers. Very fine, lacy leaves make great backgrounds

for cards. Adding other plant material in layers will complete the look.

Proportion is key to good design. Here are a few suggestions on how to achieve proportion.

Place together elements which have some feature in common.

Create major and minor areas in the design, keeping each area in harmony with, and not dominating, the others.

A subtle relationship between the elements creates a more dynamic design.

The best way to stick plant material down flat without any visible signs of glue is to use spray adhesive. Work in a well-ventilated area.

When you have selected the background card, lay the leaves out on the selected sheet of card until you are happy with the design. Then spray.

4

Trim parts of the leaves that go over the edge of the card. Use these to fill any gaps in the design. Now start to add the next layer of leaves according to your design.

5

The final card features four different leaves placed in layers on a background card. There is a balance of size and shape, plus each color is in a similar tone. Leave the card to dry before placing in an envelope.

USING EMBOSSING POWDER

Using an embossing powder to outline the shape of a rubber stamp can create super special effects on a card. Here's how to do it.

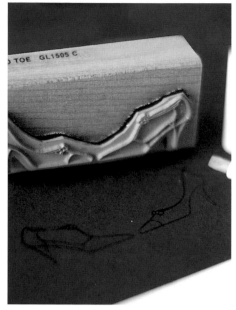

One of the more magical tools available to create a glittering effect is a clear embossing pen. The technique is easy and makes any motif, letter, or word more visually appealing.

The embossing pen contains a special slow-drying ink that gives you time to go over a stamp, write a message by hand, or draw an image by hand in preparation for sprinkling the embossing powder on top.

The powder is available in many colors, with or without glitter. Imagine a large capital letter in a scroll typeface on the card front, written first in pencil, then gone over with the embossing pen. Sprinkle a colored powder over the large letter, watch as it starts to stick to the sticky residue, then shake off the excess, and be amazed at the final effect.

Make sure you have a sheet of paper underneath to collect any excess. As with anything in craft, you can use it again.

1

Using the clear embossing pen tip, draw over the outline of the stamp. Now you can press the stamp onto the selected piece of card. The shoe design outline is faint but visible.

2

Open the container of embossing powder and tip some over the shoe outline. Do this as quickly as possible after you drew over the outline. Don't be afraid to pour it on because if you pour only a small amount, it will not stick to the outline as well. You can tip the excess back into the jar.

TIP

• *If you have not used a heat gun before, then practice this action a few times on scrap paper before using the heat gun on the final card design. This way you will avoid ruining a design and the frustration of having to do it all again!*

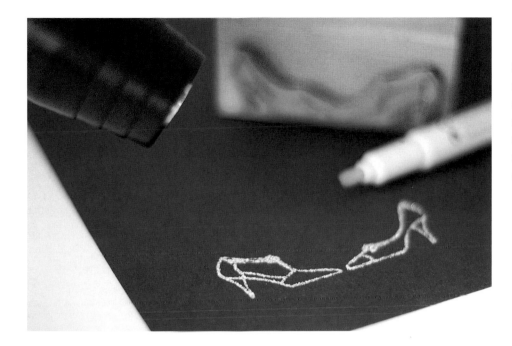

3 ————————————————

Shake off the excess embossing powder to reveal the stamp shape underneath. Use a craft heat gun over the glittery outline to seal in the embossing powder. Cover the table surface with a protective layer when using the heat gun because you do not want to damage the surface.

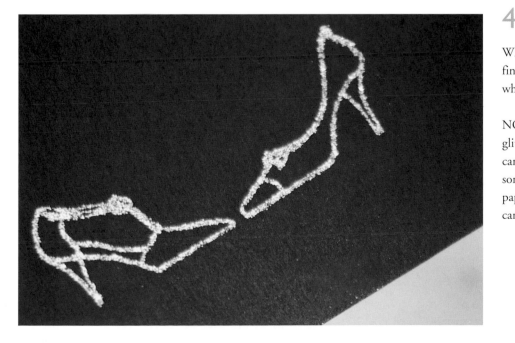

4 ————————————————

When the heat gun has done its work, the final image will be set. Now you can decide where to use it.

NOTE: You can also create several of these glittery stamp designs on the same sheet of card at the same time. If you want to use some later, wrap the card in a sheet of tissue paper. Keep it safely between a layer of flat cardboard.

INKING SOLID STAMPS

Stamps are an indispensible, quick way to make a design for a unique card. There are many designs available from craft sources. Here's how to make the most of them.

Stamps are detailed solid rubber shapes mounted on a piece of wood or a piece of hard foam. They can be embellished in many ways but the best and quickest way is to use a colored felt-tipped pen. You can also dip stamps into a tray filled with paint, but I prefer this look.

Make sure the ink soaks well into the stamp and covers all of the design. Or, if you want to produce a faded effect, you could ink one end of the image and graduate the density of the ink as you work your way toward the other end.

Stamps can be used to create some interesting designs. You can make a row vertical, horizontally, or diagonally of the same stamp outline, then add another, smaller stamp in between.

Different colored stamps can be used alternately in a design, and stamps with different patterns can also be used alternately across or up and down a card. Make the design in a random pattern for more interest.

It is up to your imagination. However, don't be too rash—remember that less is more!

1

Ink the stamp well with the tip of the pen, covering each of the designs on the surface.

2

Above you can see the flower-petal stamp has been used around an aperture to make an random pattern.

3

The finished card front. You can dress this up a little by adding a dot of all-purpose glue to the center of the flower, then adding a small bead. Leave to dry.

MAKE YOUR OWN STAMP

You will find endless hours of fun in making stamps of any shape or style. All you need is a piece of funky foam and a dark pencil.

Making your own offers many design opportunities. Each stamp will create a unique effect, and be more appreciated because you went to the trouble of doing it yourself. Buy a piece of foam from a craft supplier and draw the pattern on the surface; then cut it out. It's as simple as that.

Glue the design onto something hard such as a small block of wood, a bottle cap, or a preserving jar lid (if it is a large design)—anything that you can get a good grip on when you use the stamp to print on the card.

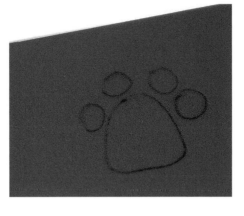

1

Using a dark pencil, draw a paw shape onto a piece of craft foam. Add toes.

2

Cut the shapes out with scissors and a sharp craft knife. Place them in the correct arrangement.

3

Add a dab of all-purpose adhesive to each foam piece and stick to the bottle cap. Use tweezers to pick up and add the pieces if they are small.

4

Using either an ink pad or a black (or colored) marker, color in the paw print. Fill in as much as you like.

5

Stamp your homemade paper onto the card. You might like to practice on another piece of scrap paper before using the stamp on the final card front.

LETTERING 101

For a special occasion card, create an individual set of letters for the card to make it unique. Here's how to do lettering over a half-circle.

Lettering is an important design tool when making a card. Usually, the style of the lettering will dictate the style of the card. A traditional type style will only look right on a card with a similar theme. The same design theory applies to modern lettering. It is best to carry through a theme and that means choosing the right look for the type as well as the embellishment.

The trend for computer-generated "handwritten" typefaces means you can have fun with words in many ways. There are lots of handwritten typefaces available and these add a whimsical appeal to any design. Some can also add humor to a card.

Experiment with lowercase letters set in a slightly uneven line across a card; a combination of lowercase and capital letters in a sentence or phrase, or large and smaller letters in a word can look interesting, as long as you keep a sense of proportion in mind. You will soon learn which typefaces you prefer.

Colored lettering can look fantastic. However, select a color that is already included in the main design. Too many colors can make for a design that is confusing for the eye to read.

I like to work with sheets of lettering that you can transfer onto a card by rubbing over individual letters evenly with a pencil.

Heavy, light, bold, broad, thin, spidery, elegant, zany, and regular lettering styles are available as rub-down lettering from art stores or websites.

If you are using an image on the front of the card, try out several type styles with it before you decide on the final style. Place the lettering next to, or under, the image and visualize its effect. Your eye will soon tell you which style is right for the general tone of the card.

3 _____

Tape the tracing paper under the trace you are using for the card. If you are using a more opaque paper for the card you may need to darken the letters so you can see the lettering through the card.

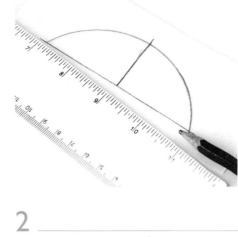

1

Place a cup on a narrow strip of paper where the arc shape needs to be, allowing space above for the lettering. Using a pencil draw, around the top half. Remove the cup.

2

Place the small piece of trace over the sheet of Letraset. Find the capital letter "T" for the first letter of the word "Thank you." Lightly outline the letter in pencil. Work your way along the half-circle with the correct letters, making sure the spacing is even across it. If the spacing looks wrong, you can tweak it to fit when you transfer the lettering.

When using lettering alone on the front of a card, you are not restricted in design. You can be as creative as you like! Some of the best cards feature just a phrase on the cover.

Some sheets of lettering feature phrases, and you may find it easier to use these than to add each letter separately. You must transfer the phrase as carefully as single letters, but this does not demand as concentration.

The main thing is to work steadily, and if you make a mistake, just start again on another of the rub-down letters over the one you messed up.

4

Begin applying the letters one by one. I prefer to use a blunt pencil to make the transfer movement even. Rub gently and keep a close eye on the spacing between the letters.

Best Dad!

In Loving Memory

Get well soon

MISSING YOU ALREADY

BON VOYAGE

SAFE JOURNEY

Just for You

the projects

ON YOUR
ENGAGEMENT

BIRTHDAY CAKE RECIPE

Here's a unique card design with a recipe
for a birthday cake to be enjoyed by everyone.

Happy Birthday

Yummy Birthday Cake

4oz sugar

4oz butter

2 eggs

4oz flour

1 tsp vanilla

*Mix together sugar and butter, then blend in eggs. Mix flour in slowly, then
add vanilla.*

*Put into two 6" sandwich tins, and cook at 375°F for 25 minutes. Cool on a
wire rack. Fill with cream and top with cream and fresh Strawberries.*

Enjoy!

The texture of the card makes this a delicious, tempting invitation to a birthday.

Type Happy Birthday, adding a scroll design
underneath. Then type your favorite recipe
underneath the scroll. Add another scroll
under the recipe (see photograph for
placement). Print, centered, onto the
parchment paper. You can also try my recipe
(opposite). Using a craft knife and the
measuring lines on the cutting mat as a
guide, cut out the words as above.

YOU WILL NEED

- Cream card blank 6½" x 4½"
  (170mm x115mm) handmade paper
- Scrap of brown wrapping paper
- Favorite cake recipe
- Small photocopied image of a cake
- Letter-sized sheet of white or faintly
  patterned parchment paper
- Rub-down type (if not using
  a computer)
- Pencil
- Glue tape
- Metal rule
- Craft knife
- Cutting mat
- Scissors

2

Using glue tape, stick the printed words to the front of the card, leaving the maximum space between for the cake image.

3

Using the craft knife and cutting mat, trim cake image to 1½" x 2¼" (40 x 55mm), then cut out a piece of brown wrapping paper ¼" (7mm) longer and wider on all sides than the finished image.

YUMMY BIRTHDAY CAKE

half cup (113g) **sugar**
half cup (113g) **butter**
2 free-range **eggs**
half cup (113g) **flour**
1 tsp **vanilla (extract)**

Mix together sugar and butter, then blend in the eggs. Mix flour in slowly, then add vanilla.
Put into two 6" (150mm) sandwich tins, and cook at 375 F for 25 minutes. Cool on a wire rack.
Frost one cake and place ontop of the other. Frost the top of this cake and top with small fresh strawberries.

Enjoy!

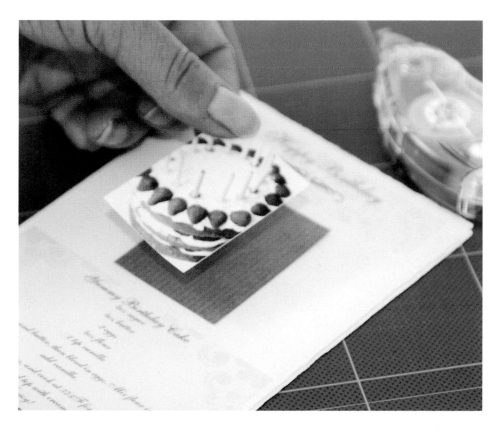

4

Stick the brown paper to the center of the card midway between both sets of words and stick the cake image on top and in the center, leaving a frame around the cake image.

A VINTAGE BIRTHDAY

Look through a collection of photographs of the person to whom
you are sending the card and select the image that shows the person at their best!
You are about to send them a blast from the past.

YOU CAN USE THIS design for a
person in the family with whom you
have a special bond, or for someone
you know will recall the moment
with pleasure. Images of the past are
are evocative and it is always good to
remind people of how it was then.

"True Friends Leave Footprints in Your Heart" is the message on this lovely card.

Photocopy a selection of old photographs, reducing their size to approximately 1¾" x 2¾" (45mm x 70mm). Using sharp scissors cut out the images and lay them on the cream card blank to see which is your favorite.

2

Cut a piece of cream card 5½" x 11" long (140mm x 280mm) to make an insert. Fold the insert in half. Lay an image onto the folded card to determine the position of the wording. Apply the wording by whichever method you have chosen.

3

Lay the photo on the card insert and establish the height you want the image to sit. Measure the halfway point of the card across, and mark lightly with a pencil. Find the center of the image the same way and mark on the reverse. Line up both pencil marks with the image level, and lightly trace around the top corners.

5

Slip the photo corners on the photograph and use them to stick the image to the translucent acetate card front at the position marked. Rub out pencil marks if necessary.

4

Insert the card into the acetate card blank using glue tape *(see Techniques, page 33)*.

A DESIGNER HANDBAG

A card for a special person that's brilliantly chic in its concept.
A girl can never have too many handbags.

Pretty in shades of pink, these handbags are eye-catching and will win over a young girl's heart.

YOU NEED A STRONG CARD FOR this because of the number of additions to its front. Also, you can use hats or shoes instead of handbags if you prefer.

1

Cut a strip of the pearl card to measure 2¼" x 5½ " (56mm x 137mm). Using glue tape, stick the card on the center front of the pink card blank.

YOU WILL NEED

- 3¼" x 6¼" (81mm x 156mm) pink card blank
- Sheet of deep rose pearlized card
- Sheet of white parchment
- ⅛" (3mm) wide satin ribbon in pale pink and deep rose
- Assortment of small pearl beads
- Rubber handbag stamp
- Stamp ink
- Watercolor paints
- Paintbrush
- Hole punch
- Glue tape
- All-purpose glue
- Pencil
- Metal ruler
- Scissors
- Craft knife
- Cutting mat

2

Ink the stamp and stamp onto the parchment *(see Techniques, page 58)*, and leave to dry. You will need to stamp four handbags in total.

3

Cut out the individual bags into 1¼" x 1½" (31mm x 37mm) rectangles and paint in the bag details using the watercolor paints. Leave to dry.

4

Using glue tape, stick three of the bags to the pearl card strip, spacing them evenly. Glue pearl beads onto the bags as bag clasps.

5

Using all-purpose glue, stick a length of ribbon down each side of the pearl card. Cut out around the outline of the last bag and punch a hole in the handle area. Thread a length of ribbon through the hole. Punch a hole in the top left-hand corner of the card, and tie the ribbon to the card through the hole, and make a knot or bow.

ROSES FOR GRANDMA

A design with roses and glitter to appreciate the life of a grandmother. The beads lift the roses, adding a glamorous sparkle.

IF YOU KNOW GRANDMA'S favorite flowers, you could substitute them for the roses, as long as the substitutions are small and delicate. Or you could use a piece of card in a contrasting color if you prefer.

1

Using the all-purpose glue, add the photograph of Grandma to the deep embossed area of the precut card.

Elegance and a quiet sophistication plus lots of love are combined in this card for Grandma.

YOU WILL NEED

- Photograph of Grandma measuring 2¼" (56mm) square
- Precut card with a de-bossed frame 6" × 8" (150mm × 200mm)
- All-purpose glue
- Tape gun
- Small beads
- Thin satin ribbon
- Tweezers
- 8 to 10 small roses

2 _____

Add the roses in small groupings around the edge of the photograph.

3 _____

Place the small beads between the roses. Dab them on with dots of glue in a random sequence. Use tweezers if you find they help you place the beads more easily.

4 _____

Add the ribbon along the crease using a tape gun. Run your finger along the edge to make sure the ribbon is firmly in place. Trim the edge neatly.

AN INVITATION

Dainty flowers send a message of affection in an invitation
that will impress the person invited for the event.

AN INVITATION SETS THE TONE
for an event, so it is important to get it
right. The flowers used on this card
indicate a cheerful occasion, one
intended to raise the spirits!

YOU WILL NEED:

- 200g card blank measuring 5¾" (145mm)
  square
- One 1¾" (43mm) square 200g white
  card for embossing template
- Three 1¾"" (43mm) squares of thin white
  160g card
- Three 1½" (35mm) 80g white paper
- Two 6" (150mm) lengths of ½" (12mm)
  wide velvet ribbon
- 16" (40cm) length of ⅛" (3mm) wide
  satin ribbon
- Large flower punch
- Small flower punch
- Pencil
- PVA glue
- Glue tape
- Embossing tool or end of paintbrush
- Metal ruler
- Craft knife
- Scissors

The layered and embossed look works well with a one-color card.

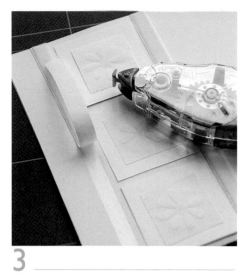

1

Using a flower punch, make a flower in the center of the thick white card square to form the embossing template. Set the flower to one side.

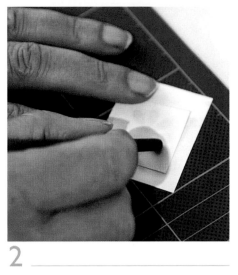

2

Using the template, emboss the flower onto the paper square. Repeat on the two other paper squares. Lay the three squares of thin white card onto the front of the card blank, placing them 1" (25mm) from the top edge, spacing them evenly apart. Glue in place.

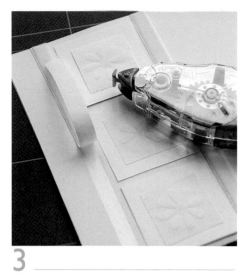

3

Using glue tape, stick an embossed square to the center of each card square. Stick a length of velvet ribbon above and below the embossed squares, using glue tape.

4

Tie the length of narrow satin ribbon around the spine of the card and knot at the top edge. Cut one end close to the top of the card and leave a longer tail on the other. Glue the punched-out flower (from Step 1) to the end of the ribbon tail using PVA glue.

5

Using the pencil, write the word "Invitation" on the bottom left-hand corner of the card. Punch a small flower out of thick card and, using PVA glue, stick it to the left of the lettering.

TIPS

• *Be meticulous when cutting and stamping*

• *Try not to get the card dirty while you work*

• *Use an envelope of a contrasting color to mail the invitation*

FOR A LOVER

Sensual thoughts are carried to a loved one with this pink lace and diamante card.

A SIMPLE DESIGN THAT conveys
the intended subtle message in an
effective way. It is made with a lace scrap
you might find in a remnant box, and
you can either write the words by hand
or use rub-down lettering. Use short
words to fit across the card.

Love is wonderful
whichever time around,
especially when the sender of
this card is such a romantic!

1

Spray mount the back of the lace in a
cardboard box. Then place the lace on a
level surface. Take the folded card and place
it in the center of the lace. Smooth the card
flat to adhere it to the lace. Fold the lace
over the top of the card. Smooth flat to
adhere. Trim the lace with scissors to sit
neatly on the edge of the card.

TIP

*Always spray the piece of paper or
card that you will be sticking to
another piece of paper. Place the
sheet of paper or card in the
bottom of a large cardboard box,
then spray. This method prevents
the adhesive from going
everywhere.*

2

Make a small rectangular strip of pink card.
Rub or write the phrase you have selected
onto the pink card, leaving a ¼" (6mm)
border all around the lettering. Add a sticky
pad to the back of the card.

3

Place the pink card in the center of the top
third of the card 1" (25mm) from the top
edge, and press in place.

4

Using all-purpose glue, add the diamantés in
the center of the lace flowers. Press firmly to
make sure they remain in place.

5

Let the card dry. Then, with the gold pen,
write your greeting with a flourish inside the
card. Let the words dry before closing to
avoid smudging the ink.

VALENTINE'S DAY

A rose and hearts on parchment paper designed to seal the friendship on a day to celebrate romance.

Fold the pink parchment like a concertina making sure the large heart template fits the fold width.

YOU WILL NEED:

- 200g card blank 4" × 8" (100mm × 200mm)
- White parchment paper
- Red parchment paper
- Pink parchment paper
- Computer, rub-down transfers, or rubber stamps with love quotes
- 12" (300mm) thin red velvet ribbon
- Small, medium, and large heart templates made from thin card
- Small heart-shaped gem
- Pencil
- Glue tape
- Hole punch
- Metal ruler
- Craft knife
- Scissors

Romance is in every word of this perfect concept for a Valentine. Red velvet ribbon provides the final touch.

"*You've got to dance like nobody's watching, dream like you will live forever, live like you're going to die tomorrow, and love like it's never going to hurt.*" *Meme Grifters*

QUOTE USED FOR THIS CARD

"You've got to dance like nobody's watching, dream like you will live forever, live like you are going to die tomorrow, and love like it is never going to hurt."

Meme Grifters

2

Place the heart template onto the folded parchment and draw around the template.

3

Hold paper layers firmly between fingers and thumb and cut out multiple hearts from folded paper. Reshape any jagged edges and erase the pencil from the top heart. Repeat steps 1, 2, and 3 with small and medium heart templates.

4

Position the two sizes of hearts randomly on the front of the card blank and stick in place with glue tape. Print "love quotes" onto the white parchment using a computer, stamps or transfers. Trim the printed parchment to 3" x 7½" (75mm x 192mm). Using glue tape stick the parchment to the front of the card covering the hearts.

5

Stick more pink hearts on top of the strip of love quotes, then punch a hole in the front of the card at the top left-hand corner.

6

Using the large heart template, cut out one shape from red parchment and punch a hole close to the center top edge. Using glue tape, attach the heart gem to the center of the punched heart.

7

Thread ribbon through the heart and the hole in front of the card. Knot the ribbon ends together to suspend the heart down the spine.

AN ENGAGEMENT GEM

An announcement of a celebration of love between two people, represented by images of the happy couple enamored of each other.

AN ENGAGEMENT CARD MEANS the moment is emotional. Using a lot of images from the life of the couple imbues the concept with memories beyond this occasion, and offers people a glimpse of both their lives so far.

1

Photocopy your images several times in black and white, reducing them in size to end up 1" (25mm) square, and age them *(see Techniques, page 53)*. Alternatively, you can do this in Photoshop on a computer.

YOU WILL NEED

- 8" × 8" (200mm x 200mm) sheet of charcoal parchment paper
- 8" × 8" (200mm x 200mm) sheet of 100gms cream paper
- Selection of 16 photos of the couple and love symbols
- Black rub-down lettering
- Small rose-tinted gem
- Glue tape
- All-purpose glue
- Pencil
- Metal ruler
- Scissors
- Craft knife
- Cutting mat

4

Stick the rose-tinted gem to the label, below the lettering, using all-purpose glue.

5

Cut a rectangle of cream paper 3¾ " x 7½" (95 x 190mm) and place it in center of back of card, using glue tape. This is where you will write the message.

The rows of images build up a picture of the lives of each person as a tribute to love.

2

Make a card blank from the parchment paper measuring 8" x 4¼" (200mm x 106mm). Arrange 16 photo tiles on the card, leaving a ¼" (6mm) border and the center of the card clear. Leave ⅛" (3mm) between each photograph. Glue tiles in place.

3

Cut a tag from cream paper measuring 2¼" x 1¼" (56mm x 30mm) and write "On Your Engagement" using rub-down letters (or write by hand) and draw a fine border around the edge using a pencil. Glue the label to the center of the card,

WEDDING BEST WISHES

White is for purity, and here it is used as the background color for a wedding card.
Lace with a scalloped edge adds a romantic touch.

YOU WILL NEED

- White card blank 5½" x 5½" (140mm x 140mm)
- Sheet of white card with pearlized finish
- 1 large diamanté bead
- ½" (12mm) wide white velvet ribbon
- Length of scalloped-edge white lace 1⅓" (33mm) wide
- 7 small pearl hearts
- Small length of silver cord
- Pencil
- All-purpose glue
- Metal ruler
- Craft knife
- Cutting mat
- Scissors
- Hole punch

1

Draw three tiers on the white card with a pencil. Use a ruler to keep the lines straight. The lower is 1⅓" deep x 4" wide (35mm x 100mm); the middle layer is 1" deep x 3" wide (25mm x 78mm), and the top layer is 1" deep x 2" wide (25mm x 50mm). Cut out the three strips. Cut lace strips the same size the card strips. Spray the back of the lace and stick to the card, smoothing it evenly.

2

Glue the card and lace strips in a tier, slightly overlapping as seen above, to form a three-tier cake. The scalloped edge gives the tiers a delicate finish. Add the small pearl hearts using dabs of all-purpose glue.

3

Place the cake about 1½" (40mm) above the lower edge and in the center of the pearlized card. Attach with sticky pads. Press firmly.

4

Attach the large diamante on top of the three-tiered cake using a small sticky pad. Press firmly.

5

Cut a heart shape from the pearlized card and punch a hole in the middle at the top. Write the initials of the couple getting married on the tag. Punch a hole at the top left-hand corner of the card. Thread the length of silver cord through the hole in the card to attach the tag as in photograph.

The final card is unique to the couple getting married.

A CUP CAKE BIRTHDAY TREAT

Here's a delightful card that will definitely
be in demand for a young person's birthday celebration.
The bead tops it off temptingly.

WHITE EYELET LACE GIVES the
impression of a paper doily on a plate,
while the white, pleated card resembles
the paper cup you would cook in.
The bead is the icing you always want
to pick off the top. This card is easy to
make and will be gratefully received.

YOU WILL NEED

- White card blank 5½" (140mm) square
- Scrap of 160g white card
- Scrap of pink felt
- Piece of eyelet lace
- Small tin can
- Pearl bead
- Spray adhesive
- Pencil
- Glue tape
- All-purpose glue
- Metal ruler
- Craft knife
- Scissors
- Cutting mat

Pink icing topped with a bead you sadly can't eat completes the design of this delightful cupcake.

1

Glue the eyelet lace to the outside of the card blank, using spray adhesive. Trim away the fabric level with the edges of the card.

2

Using a tin can as a template, draw around the base onto the felt.

3

Cut out and then trim off about a third of the felt disk, retaining the larger piece for the icing.

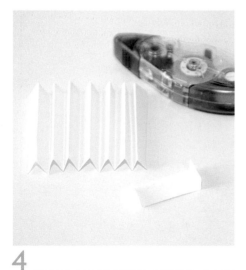

4

Cut a strip of white card 6½" x 2½" (165mm x 65mm) white and concertina across the width with approximately ½" (12mm) folds, making sure the last pleats both face in the same direction. Cut another strip of paper ½" x 2½" (12mm x 65mm) and fold over a small tab at each end.

5

Apply glue tape to the outside of the tabs and stick a tab to each side of the folded paper, close to one edge. This will make the concertina splay out to form a paper cake case. The concertina above is upside down to show how the tab is attached.

TIP

Make sure the ends of the concertina are even. You may have to cut the final end to match. Both ends should point down as in Photograph 4.

6

Stick the decorated felt icing to the front of the card with the paper case below, using all-purpose glue. Finally, stick the bead to the top of the cake for a cherry.

FINDING FISH

The fun of this card is that it is a game
when complete. Use the rod and line magnet
to catch a fish in reach!

Find a round object to use as a template,
about 2" (50mm). Using a pencil, draw two
circles onto the back of the orange card,
overlapping them by about ½" (12mm).

Gone fishing! It's one of the things that all small boys love to do, and any small boy will love this.

YOU WILL NEED

- 5½" x 8" (140mm x 200mm) card
  blank made from blue gloss card
- Letter-size sheet of orange textured
  card
- Scraps of brown card
- Scraps of white card
- Wiggly eyes
- Strong button thread
- Craft magnets
- Metal washer
- Hole punch
- Unused pencil for fishing rod
- Pencil
- All-purpose glue
- Sticky pads
- Scissors

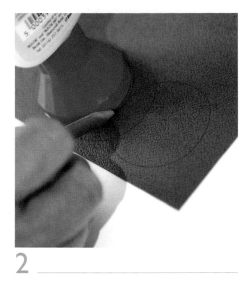

2

Place the round object on top of the second circle, lining up its edge with the edge of the first circle. Draw an arc around the object to form the tail.

3

Draw lips at the front of the first circle and cut out the fish shape. Repeat steps 1, 2, and 3 to make two more fish. Attach a wiggly eye to the front of each fish, and a magnet to the reverse side, using all-purpose glue. Let dry.

4

From the brown card cut out a few rock shapes, then, using the hole punch, punch out a few spots from the brown card, for pebbles, and white card, for air bubbles. Stick several rocks and pebbles to the base of the card to form the seabed.

5

Remove some of the tackiness from both sides of the sticky pads by dabbing them on the back of your hand quite a few times. Then use them to temporarily attach the fish to the card at the magnet positions. Once the fish are in place stick down the white spots for air bubbles.

6

Tie a length of button thread to the metal washer and wind the other end around the top of the unused pencil. Tie a firm knot to secure for the fishing line to the pencil.

TIP

To play the fishing game, remove each fish and its temporary sticky pad from the card. Lay the fish back on the card front, back in the sea!. Then use the line and its magnet to catch the fish. It's great fun for any child.

85

FOR ANY AGE

Reaching a fine age is to be celebrated with panache. This cute design
will surely make its recipient feel valued.

Cut-out daisies bring a lighthearted touch to this 60th birthday card.

HERE'S A CARD FOR ANY AGE.
This idea is based on adding an amusing
photograph of the recipient at a much
younger age than they are currently .

YOU WILL NEED

- Brown textured card blank 5½"
  (140mm) square
- Pearlized translucent paper
- Brown wrapping paper
- Old photograph of the recipient
- Gold rub-down birthday transfers
- Sheet of cream handmade paper
- Large and small daisy punches
- Pencil
- Glue tape
- Metal ruler
- Craft knife
- Cutting mat

1

Cut a 5" (125mm) square of cream
Mulberry paper and glue it to the center
front of the brown card, using glue tape.
Add the photograph on top of the paper
square, placing its lower edge slightly above
the center.

2

Cut a strip of brown wrapping paper 1" x
3½" (25mm x 90mm). Apply the gold
rub-down words and numbers to the strip.
Glue the brown label to the translucent
paper square, positioning it centered, below
the photograph.

3

Punch out a selection of large and small
daisies (about 25) from the brown wrapping
paper and the pearlized translucent paper.

Using glue tape, stick the daisies
randomly to the front of the card, placing
them over the edges of the photograph and
label. If you want, place them on the card
front first, then, when you are happy with
the way the design looks, begin to glue them
in place.

PICTURE FRAME FOR A FRIEND

A country-style card features gingham fabric and a photograph of a friend, preferably one from when the friend was very young!

THE CLEVER ASPECT OF THIS card is you can take the photograph with the metal frame off the card and place it on display on a bookshelf or mantelpiece. It's a gift and a card in one!

YOU WILL NEED:

- Precut tri-fold cream card 6" x 8" (150 x 200mm)
- Piece of gingham fabric 4" x 6" (100mm x 150mm)
- Small piece aluminum foil ¹⁄₁₆" (1mm) thick
- Old photograph 2⅜" (60mm) square
- Diamond heart
- Old ballpoint pen (no ink)
- Pencil
- Glue dots
- Sticky pads
- Metal ruler
- Pinking shears
- Cutting mat
- Spray adhesive

Well, aren't I as cute as a button framed in decorative foil?

1

Place the piece of gingham fabric in the middle of the third section of the card. Line up the aperture over the gingham. Then turn the aperture flap back and spray with adhesive. Close this down onto the gingham. Flatten evenly and put to one side.

2

With a ruler and a pencil, draw a square with 3½"(90mm) sides on the sheet of foil. Cut along the line with the pinking shears to make a decorative edge.

3

With the end of the empty ballpoint pen, make a dot on each of the scallops.

6

Stick a glue dot to the back of the heart. Place the heart at the center of the bottom of the frame. Add sticky pads top and bottom on the back of the framed photo and attach to the gingham, using the lines of the gingham to make sure it is on square.

Using all-purpose glue, attach the edges of the gingham to the inside of the aperture. Press firmly in place.

4

Take the photo and place it in the middle of the foil square. Attach two sticky pads to the back of the photograph and stick in place.

5

Take the ruler and make a frame around the photo, using a pencil, then make another frame about ⅛" (3mm) away from the first frame. Join the edges of the frame neatly.

AN EASTER EXTRAVAGANZA

When it is time to acknowledge the joy of Spring and Easter eggs, capture that feeling with this colorful card, a floral tribute to the new season.

I

Fold the sheet of orange parchment in half across the width to make a card blank 5½" x 8½" (140mm x 212mm).

Bright yellow and white daisies make an appealing picture for Easter.

2

Cut two 1" x 5½" (25mm x 140mm) strips of yellow parchment. Using the small daisy punch, make a line of evenly spaced daisies along the center of each strip. Put these to one side. Using glue tape, stick a strip down each side of the card front.

3

Punch out six large daises from the yellow parchment. Then spell out the word "Easter" by rubbing down a single letter into the center of each daisy.

TIP

You can also use a baby chick punch or an Easter Bunny punch for this card.

5

Punch three large white daisies from white paper and three dots from the yellow parchment. Stick the yellow dots to the daisy centers. With two of the retained yellow punched-out daisies, make a daisy chain of white and yellow daisies, using small spots of glue on the tip of a petal.

4

Arrange the large daises down the card's center panel in a zigzag manner, spelling out the word "Easter." Stick down the daisies, using dots of PVA glue. Punch out some white dots, using the hole punch, and stick to the centers of the small punched-out daisies.

6

Punch a small hole through the center of the top daisy and thread the length of ribbon through it. Wrap the ribbon around the front of the card close to the spine and secure the ends together on the inside with a piece of sticky tape. The daisy chain will swing freely from the top of the card.

IT'S CHRISTMAS!

A tree is one of the most recognized symbol
of Christmas, and here it adds sparkle
as a celebration of the winter season.

A NONTRADITIONAL COLOR
for this Christmas card's background, yet
the tree outline, the silver, and the
sparkly gems are evocative of a bright
starry night in winter.

1

Open out the card blank and draw a border
¾" (20mm) all around on the front cover.
Then cut out the center of the card to make
the aperture.

Blue and silver are a nontraditional christmas combination, but it works well with the design.

YOU WILL NEED:

- Blue card blank 5½" (140mm) square
- Sheet of thin acetate
- Silver contour glass paint
- White glass paint
- Paint-brush
- Scrap paper for template
- Sparkly gems (optional)
- Pencil
- Glue tape
- Sticky tape
- Metal ruler
- Craft knife
- Cutting mat
- Scissors

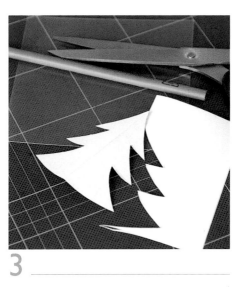

2 _____

Using the craft knife and measuring lines on the cutting mat as a guide, cut out a 4¾" (120mm) square of acetate.

3 _____

Fold the scrap piece of paper in half and draw the outline of half a tree and its branches up to the folded edge, about 3" (75mm) tall. Cut out the tree from the folded paper and open the tree out to form the template.

4 _____

Temporarily stick the template to center of the acetate using sticky tape. Turn over the acetate and trace around the edge of the tree using the glass contour paint. Add dots around the tree to represent snowflakes and draw a star at the top of the tree. Leave the paint to dry overnight.

5 _____

The next day, remove the template from the back of the acetate and, using the brush, fill in the center of the tree with white glass paint. Leave to dry as before.

6 _____

The next day, using glue tape, stick the acetate in the center of the back section of the blue card aperture. If you want, decorate the top of the tree with a sparkly gem, and paint the branches with tiny baubles.

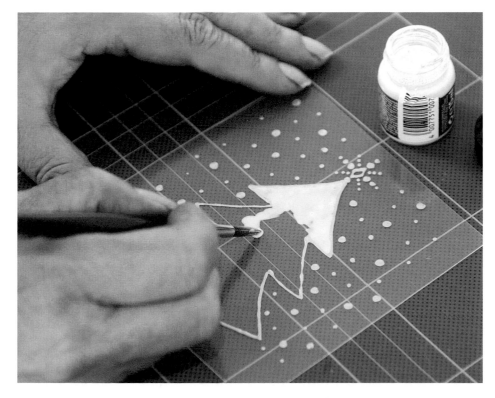

TIME TO PARTY

There's no mistaking the message of this enticing card:
get yourself ready for a great night out.

THIS CARD WAS INSPIRED by a scrap of red and white polka-dot fabric I found at home. When it was laid against the white card, the design came to me.

1 ————————————

Using the tape glue, stick a length of the ribbon to the top and bottom edges of the card blank, leaving a small margin.

2 ————————————

Cut a strip of white paper 2¾" x 7½" (70 x 190mm). Using spray adhesive, stick it to the polka-dot fabric.

YOU WILL NEED:

- 6" × 8" (150 x 200mm) white card blank
- Sheet of 100gms paper
- Scrap of red textured card
- Scrap of white card
- Scrap of red polka dot cotton fabric
- Two 6" (150mm) lengths of red polka dot ribbon, ½" (10mm) wide
- Rubber high-heel shoe stamp
- Clear embossing pen
- Silver embossing powder
- Large daisy punch
- Rub-down "Your Special Day" words in gold
- Heat gun
- Needle and thread
- Spray adhesive
- Glue tape
- Sticky pads
- Pencil
- Metal ruler
- Scissors
- Craft knife
- Cutting mat

Red and white promise a delightful evening ahead. This is the way to entice people to party!

3

Concertina the fabric-covered paper in ½" (12mm) folds, making sure that the first and last pleats are folded to the paper side. Trim if necessary to get the correct pleating.

4

Using the needle and thread gather up one pleated edge of the folded paper, to form the waist of the skirt and tie off the thread ends.

5

Cut a small piece of white card approx. 2¾" x 1¾" (70 x 45mm) and fold it in half. Draw half a dress bodice up to the fold, shaping in the waist, and drawing a "sweetheart" neckline. Cut this shape out from the folded paper. Open out the template and use it to cut out a bodice from red textured card. From the remaining red card cut one 1" x 2" (25 x 50mm) strip for a label and write or rub down the words "Your Special Day" in gold fancy type.

8

Stick the shoes in the bottom left-hand corner of card, using glue tape. Stick the bodice to the skirt using a sticky pad. Then, using more pads, stick the dress to the card on the diagonal. Punch out a white daisy and, using glue tape, stick it to the top right-hand corner of the label. Attach the daisy label to the top left-hand corner of the card with a sticky mount, lining up its edge with the toe of the outermost shoe.

6

Lay the bodice onto a scrap of paper and, using the embossing pen, draw in the bodice seams and around the edges. Sprinkle over embossing powder and tap off any excess. Use the heat gun to set the powder.

7

Ink over the details on the rubber stamp using the embossing pen. Stamp onto the red card, sprinkle with silver embossing powder, and tap off any excess. Use the heat gun to set the powder. Cut out the shoe shapes.

THINKING OF YOU

Here's a concept to use as a sophisticated card for any special occasion.
It uses the pattern in the wallpaper as the basis for the design.

THE KEY IS IN FINDING A section of the wallpaper design that you like. Make a thin picture frame (from scrap card) and place this over different parts of the wallpaper to help you decide which part of the pattern to use. Using scissors, cut the area of the pattern out and remove the temporary frame.

YOU WILL NEED

- Sheet of wallpaper offcut
- Letter-sized sheet of white card
- 5 beads to match a color in the wallpaper
- Thin craft wire
- Diamanté
- Length of thin black ribbon
- Needle and black thread
- Glue tape
- Spray adhesive
- Metal ruler
- Cutting mat
- Craft knife
- Pencil
- Scissors

I

Place the white card on a cutting mat, then lay the wallpaper on top. Pencil around the wallaper, then cut it out using scissors. This piece is the front and back of the card.

2

Fold the white card in half, making a tall, portrait shape. Spray the back of the wallpaper, then stick it to the card. Using a ruler, trim the wallpaper and card neatly.

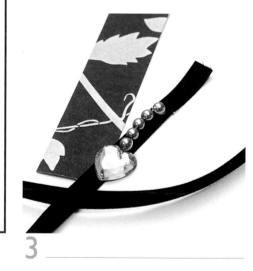

3

Thread five beads onto a small length of wire then add the diamante on the end. Sew the beads to the black ribbon firmly so they will not unravel.

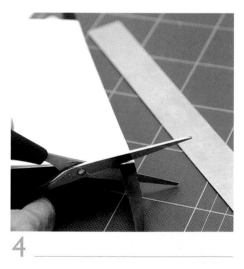

4

Using glue tape, stick the ribbon to the front of the card, exactly on the spine, with the beads and diamante at the top of the card. Leave to dry. Trim any extra ribbon.

FOR A BEST FRIEND

A vintage-style card features a photograph of you and your friend
on a memorable occasion.

THE MAGNET ON THE BACK OF
the old photograph turns this into a
refrigerator magnet! You can personalize
the words; just follow the process out-
lined below, writing the words by hand
or typing them on a computer.

YOU WILL NEED

- Piece of textured card measuring
  8" x 8½ " (200mm x 212mm) tall
- Photograph measuring 3" x 2½"
  (75mm x 60mm) tall
- Self-adhesive magnet
- Ink pen for writing *or* a computer
- Letter-size sheet white paper
- Metal ruler
- Craft knife
- 1 teaspoon instant coffee in water
- Cotton wool ball/tissue
- Sticky pads
- Glue tape
- Scissors
- Paper towel
- Cutting mat

This card features a lovely
combination of a photograph
and inspirational text.

1

Fold the card in half vertically. Stick the magnet to the back of the photograph, across the center.

2

On a computer, set up a text box 3" x 3" (75mm x 75mm). Add a border as a guide for cutting out later. Leave ½" (12mm) margin all round. In a large type size, write "A Friend Is a Present You Give Yourself". Under this, in a smaller type size, write "Robert Louis Stephenson." Print this out on plain white paper. Cut out inside the border line to make sure all the edges are straight.

3

Create a second text box 3" x ⅞" (80mm x 20mm). This goes above the photograph and contains the words "Best Friend", either handwritten or typed. Allow a ⅓" (8mm) gap between the text and the edge of the parchment paper. Trim to size evenly.

4

With a piece of paper towel lightly dipped in the cold coffee mixture, gently dab the words on the strips. This gives an aged effect to the paper. Build up the color gradually. You can always add more, but you cannot take it away. Leave to dry.

5

Trim the "Best Friend" strip to the width of the photograph. Glue it above the photograph, centered, and ¾" (18mm) from the top edge of the card.

CHRISTENING A BABY

Softly, softly mark the important ceremonial occasion with this appropriate card, accented with a small lace bow.

A CARD THAT BECOMES A bookmark! You could adapt this design for other momentous events, too.

The front panel of this card becomes a bookmark and is something to keep forever.

YOU WILL NEED

- 4" x 8½" (100mm x 212mm) white card blank
- Sheet of acetate ⅛" 3mm thick
- 1½" x 2" (35 x 50mm) black and white photo of the baby
- Letter-size sheet of white paper (80g)
- Letter-size sheet of pearlized paper
- Ribbon bow
- Length of ⅛" (3mm) wide white satin ribbon
- Length of ⅛" (5mm) wide silver lamé ribbon
- Silver contour glass paint
- White glass paint
- Paintbrush
- Hole punch
- Glue tape
- Pencil
- Metal ruler
- Scissors
- Craft knife
- Cutting mat
- All-purpose glue

1

Cut a piece of pearlized paper 3½" x 8" (90 x 200) and center it on the front of the white card blank. Glue in place.

2

Cut a strip of acetate for the bookmark measuring 7" x 1½" (180 x 40mm) and punch a hole in the middle of one short end.

3

To make a paper template: using a pencil, trace around the acetate bookmark onto the white paper and draw around the punched hole. Measure the halfway point along the top and bottom edges on the template and draw a line top to bottom in the center to connect the two points. Draw an arc at the top and write the baby's new name along it *(see Techniques page 60)*. Draw a heart below. Mark the position where the photo is to be placed (in the center). Then write the date of the christening below and add another heart. Your template is now ready.

4

Secure the acetate bookmark over the paper template. Using the silver contour glass paint, trace over the words and around the outlines of the hearts. Leave to dry.

5

Fill in the hearts using the white glass paint. Leave to dry.

6

Glue the photograph in place, attach the ribbon bow below, and tie a satin ribbon bow through the punched hole at the top.

7

Punch a hole in the center of the top edge of the card blank approx. ½" (15mm) down. Lay the bookmark on top of the card, lining up the holes. Thread a short length of silver lamé ribbon through the holes and secure the ends together on the inside of the card with glue tape.

FOR A NEW-BORN BABY

Announcing the birth of a baby is an important occasion. Friends will adore this delicately colored card, as baby will, too, when he or she grows up.

Matching buttons make a fine pair of wheels on this traditional pram for a new-born baby.

AN IMPRESSIVE CARRIAGE WITH cute pearly buttons with blue trim for wheels uses inking and bleaching techniques to create the visual effects.

1

Using the pinking shears, trim a thin strip of white card from one of its short sides and place it to one side.

YOU WILL NEED

- 6⅓" x 5" (160mm x 125mm) white card blank
- Letter-size sheet of white card
- Letter-size sheet of pale blue card
- Pinking shears
- Two ¾" (18mm) diameter blue buttons
- Length of ⅛" (3mm) wide blue Satin ribbon
- Blue ink
- Bleach
- Large paintbrush
- Hole punch
- Glue tape
- Pencil
- Scissors
- Tin can

2

Ink (top) and bleach (above) the remaining part of the sheet of white card *(see Techniques, page 50).*

3

Before the dyed card starts to dry, tear it across the width to create a jagged edge. Do this carefully because if you rip along the edge too quickly, the paper might tear in the wrong direction and you will have to start all over again. Leave the card to dry.

4

Using a tin can as a template cut out a circle from the pale blue card. Cut circle exactly in half and use one piece for the carriage base. Cut the remaining half of the circle in half again and retain one piece for the hood and trim a ¼" (6mm) curved strip from the outer edge of the other for the handle.

6

Assemble the pram and glue it to the center of the card blank, overlapping the bleached section. Use glue tape for this step.

5

Choose the best-looking section of the inked and bleached torn card and lay it over half of the front of the card blank. Stick in place with glue tape and trim the piece level with the card edges. Retain the scraps.

7

Cut a length of blue ribbon to hang the tag. Cut a strip of the scalloped strip to fit horizontally along the carriage top, using glue tape. Cut another strip of the pinked edge of the card to fit the front of the carriage hood and stick in place. Glue the buttons below the carriage to represent wheels.

8

Punch a hole in the top left-hand corner of the card. Cut a tag from the bleached card scraps 2" x 1" (50 x 25mm), placing the jagged edge at one short end. Trim the other short end and punch in a hole. Thread a length of blue ribbon through the tag. Write the baby's name on it, and tie to the top of the card through the punched hole. Knot the ribbon ends together.

HAPPY MOTHER'S DAY

This heart-shaped foil tribute to Mom can be taken off the card and hung in a special place around the home.

Mom stands out when witten in tin foil. She will be pleased at the effort you have made.

104

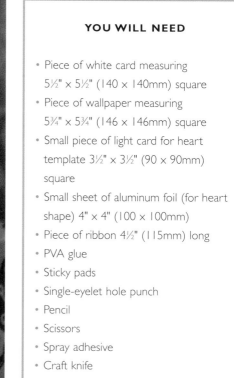

I

Cut a piece of wallpaper to cover front and back of the white card. Spray the back of the wallpaper and mount onto the card. Trim to fit neatly.

YOU WILL NEED

- Piece of white card measuring 5½" x 5½" (140 x 140mm) square
- Piece of wallpaper measuring 5¾" x 5¾" (146 x 146mm) square
- Small piece of light card for heart template 3½" x 3½" (90 x 90mm) square
- Small sheet of aluminum foil (for heart shape) 4" x 4" (100 x 100mm)
- Piece of ribbon 4½" (115mm) long
- PVA glue
- Sticky pads
- Single-eyelet hole punch
- Pencil
- Scissors
- Spray adhesive
- Craft knife

2

Make a heart from a piece of paper measuring 3½" (90mm) square. Fold the paper in half, then cut out a half a heart shape. Open it out and trim.

3

Place the card heart on the square of metal and draw around the heart shape with a pencil.

4

Make a hole at the top of the heart using a hole punch.

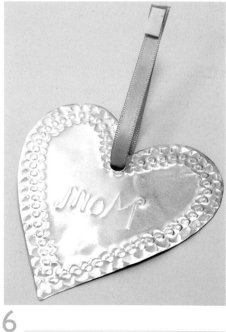

5

Draw a scallop edge around the heart with a pencil. Add circles below the scallops to create a lace edge effect. Lightly trace the word 'Mom'. When pleased with the look, press hard to write the word onto the metal.

6

Thread the ribbon through the hole in the heart. Glue the two ends together, one over the other. Cut a thin strip of sticky pad and attach it to the ribbon, then attach the ribbon to the front of the card.

CELEBRATE FATHER'S DAY

Wallpaper is the star of this card, with its stripes and texture. This could be a birthday, or work as a Father's Day card.

1

Fold the selected wallpaper along a stripe to get a straight edge.

2

Fold the sheet of white card in half and place inside the folded wallpaper to ensure the size of the wallpaper matches the card.

3

Cut the wallpaper to just over the size of the card. Using spray adhesive, spray the wrong side of the folded wallpaper. Take the cream card and tip it into the folded spine of the wallpaper.

Dad will loe the sentiment in this card.

YOU WILL NEED

- Sheet of gray card 1¾" x 6" (45mm x 150mm)
- Letter-size sheet plain white card
- Wallpaper offcut in blue pattern
- Letter-size sheet of white paper
- 2 buttons to match wallpaper color
- Metal ruler
- Craft knife
- Pencil
- Cutting mat
- Glue tape
- Glue dots or sticky pad
- Silver or gold pen

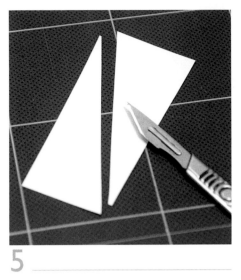

4

Flatten one side of the card to the wallpaper and smooth it. Repeat this on the other side. Open the card out and smooth over the wallpaper, adhering it to the card. Using a craft knife and ruler, trim the wallpaper to the exact edge of the card. Leave to dry.

5

Cut the white paper into a rectangular shape measuring 1¼" x 3¼" (31mm x 80mm). Using a craft knife, cut in half diagonally to make the two collars.

6

Cut a square of the striped wallpaper for the pocket.

To make the handkerchief

Cut a piece of white card into the shape in the photograph, measuring 1½" (37mm) across the top, each side measuring 2" (50mm), and the lower edge measuring 1¼" (31mm).

To assemble the tie

Match each pointed end of the white card pieces to each of the top corners of the card. Make sure they meet in the center of the card. Glue in place using the glue tape. Glue the tie in position, then use glue dots to place the buttons, one above the other, underneath the tie. Follow the positioning seen in the main photograph if you are having a problem.

7

Using glue tape, stick the pocket, with the stripes horizontal, about ¼" (6mm) from the bottom on the right-hand side. With a silver or black pen, write the words "Best Dad" on the white card handkerchief, then slip it inside the pocket.

BON VOYAGE & GOOD LUCK

All packed and ready to go! All you need is the card to wish the traveler
good luck and a safe journey home.

An inspired design that will bring good luck to the traveler.

DESIGNED TO LOOK LIKE A
suitcase complete with luggage stickers,
this is a great card design. It is simple to
make, and you can have fun with the
stickers and the tags.

YOU WILL NEED

- Brown leather-effect card blank 6" x 8"
  (150mm x 200mm)
- Scraps of different colored card
- Two 8" (150mm) lengths of ⅓" (10mm)
  wide striped Petersham ribbon
- Luggage label
- Rub-down letters
- Daisy punch
- Thin string
- Pinking shears
- Glue tape
- Metal ruler
- Craft knife
- Scissors

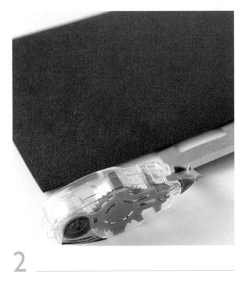

1

Cut a 2½" (65mm) square of pale brown scrap card, fold in half and draw a line about ½" (12mm) in from the folded edge and the two short side edges. Cut out along pencil lines to form a handle as in the photograph below. You are making a joined double L-shape.

2

Stick handle to the spine of the card blank in the center, using glue tape.

3

Make luggage labels. Cut out various shapes from the colored cards, using both plain scissors and pinking shears. Punch out a few daisies from the shapes and add words using the rub-down letters. Add "Bon Voyage" to the luggage label, using the rub-down letters.

4

Lay the two lengths of ribbon down each side of the "suitcase", placing them 1" (25mm) in from each side edge. Stick only the ends of the ribbon in place, using the glue tape.

5

Slip the luggage labels under the loose part of the ribbons and stick in place with glue tape. To finish, tie the luggage label around the handle at the top, using thin string.

A RUBY WEDDING ANNIVERSARY

Marking a momentous event is a tribute to the people involved. Make this your personal acknowledgment of a marriage that's lasted forty years!

THE CONCEPT CAN BE USED for a couple who have been married for any number of years *(see the list of anniversaries on the opposite page)*. Just change the color of the hearts to match the anniversary—for example, silver hearts for a silver wedding anniversary.

YOU WILL NEED:

- 4½" × 8¼" (115 × 210mm) card blank with a 2¼" × 3" (56 × 75mm) aperture, made from pearlized card
- Thin cellophane bag
- Red heart confetti
- Gold glitter
- Red heart gem
- A length of fancy-edged white organza ribbon
- A length of ⅛" (3mm) wide gold lamé ribbon
- Gold rub-down lettering
- Glue tape
- Pencil
- Scissors

Sip a ruby-red champagne cocktail to celebrate the 40th anniversary, while you admire the hearts in the clear cellophane bag.

1

Sprinkle a little glitter into the clear cellophane bag, plus a few red confetti hearts. Fold over the top flap and, using extra glue tape, close it firmly to ensure an airtight seal.

2

Attach the bag to back of the aperture in the card, using glue tape along the top and side edges. Make sure the base of the bag sits as close to the lower edge of the window as possible. Then the confetti will not be hidden behind the card.

3

Run a strip of glue tape down the spine of the card and stick on the gold lamé ribbon. Butt the organza ribbon up to the gold ribbon and stick down. Trim the ends of the ribbons level with the top and bottom edges of the card.

4

Write the word "Ruby" elegantly in the lower right-hand corner using the gold rub-down letters. Using glue tape, add the heart gem to the right of the word.

IMPORTANT ANNIVERSARIES

5 years	Wood
10 years	Tin/Aluminum
15 years	Crystal
20 years	China
25 years	Silver
30 years	Pearl
35 years	Coral/Jade
40 years	Ruby
45 years	Sapphire
50 years	Gold
55 years	Emerald
60 years	Diamond

A NEW HOME

Brown card and corrugated cardboard combine with gingham for this design. Fill all the windows with the same person, or have different people in each.

We've moved! Guess who is in the window peeping out at you? The author and her partner.

1

From the scrap paper cut a rectangle 4" x 5½" (100mm x 140mm). Fold it in half across its width. Draw a diagonal line from corner to corner and cut out the shape. This is the template for a triangular roof.

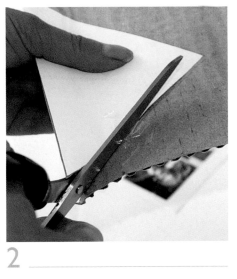

2

Lay the template on the reverse side of the corrugated cardboard making sure the ridges run horizontally across the roof. Temporarily hold the template in place, using sticky tape, and cut out the shape.

3

Measure 2¾" (70mm) down from the top of the card blank and draw a pencil line parallel to the top edge. Line up the base of the corrugated roof with the horizontal pencil line and glue in place. Trim the card to match the diagonal roof edges.

4

Cut out four 1½" (41mm) squares from the white card and one front door, measuring 1" x 2" (25mm x 50mm) from the pink card. Position these windows and the door on the front of the card (see main photograph for positioning). Use glue tape to stick them in place.

5

Photocopy the photographs of the moving people to get a passport-sized image. Using scissors, cut out each person's head and shoulders silhouette. Using glue tape, stick their images to the center of the windows.

6

Cut a rectanglar template for curtains measuring 1½" x ¾" (40mm x 20mm) using scrap paper. Cut corner to corner to make two triangles. Use the template to cut four pairs of curtains from gingham. Use glue tape to stick curtains in place over faces.

7

To finish with a flourish, glue the bead to the door for a doorknob. Create window boxes or decorate around the door with punched-out flowers or ribbon roses.

CONGRATULATIONS

This is the ideal card for letting a young ballerina know how proud you are of her when she passes her ballet examinations. It's a pretty card, too.

THE THEME OF THIS CARD is very feminine. However, you can easily change the garment hanging on the small coat hanger to a masculine football jersey or a golf sweater, and change the tulle for a cotton in the colors of the sports team.

YOU WILL NEED

- 5½" × 8½ (140 × 212mm) pearlized card blank
- Scrap of pink netting
- Scrap of pink paper
- Small ribbon bow
- Small pink bead
- Scrap of white card for template
- Pink rub-down lettering
- Silver beading wire
- Round-nosed pliers
- Needle and thread
- Pencil
- All-purpose adhesive
- Sticky pads
- Scissors

Delicately colored and feminine in its design, this pretty card is made from items you might already have at home.

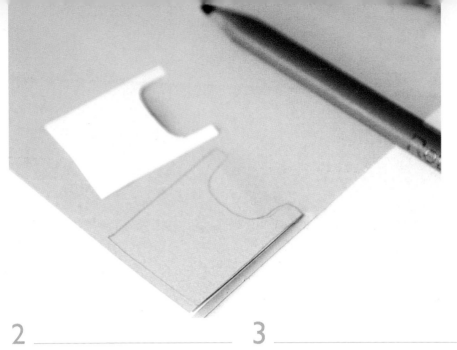

1

Cut a strip of netting 3" x 10" (75mm x 260mm) and work a row of gathering stitches along one of the long edges. Pull up the gathers tightly and fasten off.

2

Cut a piece of white card about 1" x 1½" (25 x 37mm) and fold in half. Draw half a dress bodice up to the fold and cut it out from the folded paper. Open the template out and use to make a small bodice from the pink paper.

3

Using all-purpose adhesive, stick the bodice to the gathered edge of the net skirt.

4

Cut a ¾" (18mm) length of beading wire. Using the pliers, shape the wire into a mini clothes hanger. Thread the bead onto the clotheshanger hook and neatly trim away any excess wire.

5

Glue the dress straps to the coat hanger and the ribbon bow to the waist of the dress. *(See main photograph.)* Leave to dry. Attach the dress to the center of the card front, using sticky pads on the bodice.

6

When the card is assembled, rub down the word "Congratulations" directly onto the card, about 1¾" (43mm) down from the top edge, above the coathanger and the dress. Center the word on the front of the card. Use a ruler as a guide to align the letters of the word as you work across the card from left to right.

GET-WELL WISHES

The thought does count when you are not feeling well, so when you know of someone who needs a lift, make this caring card for them.

SHADES OF LAVENDER with a bunch of fresh or dried lavender attached to the front of the card make for an interesting get-well card.

I ⎯⎯⎯⎯⎯⎯⎯⎯⎯⎯⎯⎯⎯

Fold the lavender card in half and trim to make a 5½" (140mm) square card blank. Retain the remaining section of the card.

YOU WILL NEED

- Letter-sized sheet of lavender card 1½" (40cm) of ⅛" (3mm) wide deep lavender ribbon
- Few short sprigs fresh or dried lavender
- White rub-down or sticky dots
- White rub-down lettering
- Sticky pads
- Pencil
- Metal ruler
- Scissors
- Craft knife
- Cutting mat

A lovely bunch of healing lavender makes an appealing addition to a get-well card. The small tag is a sweet touch.

2

Rub down the white dots randomly over the front of the card blank.

3

Wrap the ribbon around the lavender stems several times and finish in a bow. Trim the ribbon ends diagonally to stop them from fraying. Cut the lavender stems level to finish approximately 4¼" (110mm) long.

TIP

Write a special message to your unwell friend or relative on the little tag. The recipient can remove the lavender as a keepsake.

Generally regarded as the most useful essence for medicinal and therapeutic purposes, lavender is a good antiseptic as well. The essence was widely used by the Romans in bathing spas.

4

Attach the bunch of lavender diagonally to the card front using a sticky mount. Place the bunch about 1" (25mm) from the spine of the card, letting the bunch cover as much of the card as it needs to.

5

Make a 1½" x 2½" (40 x 62mm) folded tag from the retained section of the lavender card. Write the words "Get well soon" on the front of the tag using the rub-down letters. Attach the tag to the bottom right-hand corner of the card with a sticky pad.

SAY THANK YOU

A floral theme for this gracious card sends
kind thoughts with style. Its transparent
quality adds an ethereal elegance.

A FLORAL THEME FOR THIS
thank-you card is simple in its concept.
The lettering requires concentration, but
other than that, it is a delight to make.
The embroidered fabric and the stamped
flowers emphasize the delicacy of the
card's design.

YOU WILL NEED

- Letter-size sheet white parchment
  paper
- Letter-sized sheet of 160g card
- Scrap of pearlized card
- Eyelet lace fabric
- Length of shirring elastic
- Length of ⅛" (3mm) white ribbon
- Two white shirt buttons
- White rub-down letters
- Large daisy punch
- Pencil
- Glue tape
- Spray adhesive
- Hole punch
- Metal ruler
- Craft knife
- Cutting mat
- Scissors

Transparent parchment paper combines well with the light embroidered fabric and stamped flowers.

1

Measure a quarter of the length of one side of the parchment paper and mark the place with a pencil dot. Fold the parchment across its width to this mark. Then fold the other end of the paper so they both meet at the center as shown above. Trim the folded parchment down to make a square card. Retain the cut-off section.

2

Trim the eyelet lace to the size of the cut-off parchment paper. Using spray adhesive, spray the back of the lace and stick it to the cut-off parchment. Trim away the excess fabric from around the parchment. Glue the lace and parchment strip around the bottom of the main card. Trim to fit exactly.

3

Punch out four daisies from the pearlized card. Punch a hole in the center of each. Cut a ¾" (18mm) length of elastic, thread the ends through the holes in each button, then pull through the holes in the centers of two daisies. Repeat with the second button.

5

Using a pencil, mark the center position of the daisy fasteners along the front opening edges of the card at ¼" (6mm) in from the edge. Punch a hole at each mark. Thread the daisy elastic through and tie a double knot at the back to secure, not too tightly to the card, as you will wind the ribbon beneath each flower to bring the card fronts together.

7

Apply rub-down letters in an arc across the top of the card, using a template *(see Techniques, page 61)*.

8

Cut a 5" (125mm) square of thin card and glue onto the inside card back. Wind the ribbon around both daisies to loosely close the card.

PET SYMPATHY

The demise of a beloved pet can be traumatic. I hope this card brings back happy memories of the dearly departed.

Stamp black paw prints randomly over the front of the card blank.

The dog collar, the dog tag, a leash, a bone, and the paw prints convey a message of sympathy.

YOU WILL NEED

- 5½"(140mm) square blue card blank
- Letter sheet 160g dark brown card
- Scrap blue card
- Craft foil
- Paw stamp (shop-bought or home-made, see Techniques, page 59)
- Stamp ink
- 2 jewelery findings
- Medium-sized acrylic gems
- 8" (200mm) of black Russia braid
- Black rub-down lettering
- Hole punch
- Glue tape
- All-purpose glue
- Pencil
- Metal ruler
- Scissors
- Craft knife
- Cutting mat

2

Cut a strip of brown card about 1¼" x 8" (30 x 200mm). Punch a small hole at the center point along one long edge. Loop the strip around and, using glue tape, stick each end of the collar to the front of the card as above. Attach the gems to collar using all-purpose adhesive. Leave to dry.

3

Trace a circle around a cotton bobbin onto the foil. Cut out using scissors. Punch a small hole at the top. Using a pencil, write the name of the deceased dog on the foil. Attach to the collar through the center hole with the jewelery finding.

FOR A KITTY

If your friend's cat has passed away, you can use velvet ribbon to cover the collar and attach a small bell.

4

Cut a strip of blue card 2¾" x 1" (70 x 25mm) and write "In Loving Memory" on the strip using the rub-down letters. Rule a fine pencil line around the edge to make a border. Using glue tape, stick the strip to the bottom right-hand corner of the card.

5

Draw a dog's bone onto another piece of craft foil, about 1½" x 1" (37mm x 25mm) in size, and cut out with scissors. Punch a small hole at the center of the bone and attach a jewellery finding. Thread a length of the Russia braid through the finding.

6

Punch a hole in the top left-hand corner of the card. Thread both ends of the braid through the hole, from front to back, leaving a small loop at the front to emulate a dog collar, with the bone hanging from it. Cut off one end of the braid, leaving a short length, and fasten down with sticky tape on the inside.

7

Make a loop in the remaining end of the braid, to form a handle for the dog leash. Wrap a small strip of foil around the braid to bind the end in place. Trim the foil and braid ends to neaten.

IN SYMPATHY

A loved one has passed away, and this bereavement card will be much appreciated as a token of your affection for the family.

THE OUTLINES OF DRIED flowers show through an acetate window in this design. Pale blue flowers match the blue translucent parchment paper. You can change the color of the flowers, as long as you keep within the pale shades.

Delicate dried flowers sit between acetate to make the design of this sympathy card.

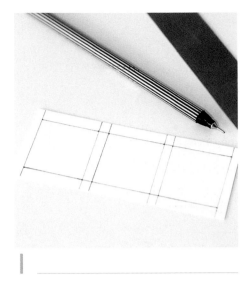

1

To make a template from the white card for the acetate windows, cut a strip of card 5" x 2" (125 x 50mm). Starting at one end of the strip, measure and make marks along both long edges as follows: ¼" (6mm), 1¼" (30mm), ¼"(6mm), 1¼" (30mm), ¼" (6mm), 1¼" (30mm) and ¼" (6mm). Using the ruler, join the marks across the strip as shown in the photograph above.

2

Measure down both short ends of the strip and mark as follows: ¼" (6mm), 1¼" (30mm) and ¼" (3mm). Join the marks along the length of the end strips.

3

Lay the template under the front of the card blank, placing it close to, and parallel to, the spine. Using a pencil and ruler, trace around the three square window shapes.

4

Cut out windows using a craft knife and cutting mat. Cut two strips of acetate 5" x 2" (125 x 50mm). Stick one strip to inside of windows using all-purpose glue. Place a dried flower in each window and glue in place using all-purpose glue.

5

Stick the second strip of acetate to front of card covering windows and flowers, using a dot of glue in each corner.

YOU WILL NEED

- 5" (125mm) square card blank made from blue parchment paper
- Scrap of blue parchment paper
- Sheet of thin acetate
- White rub-down letters
- White card for template
- Dried flowers
- Pencil or pen
- All-purpose glue
- Metal ruler
- Scissors
- Craft knife
- Cutting mat

TIP

Trim the edges of each of the dried flowers neatly so they do not look straggly. Select a color that soothes, and a type of flower that has a visually gentle form. Something fragile is excellent for this card.

6

Cut a strip of blue parchment 1¼" x 3½" (30 x 90mm). Rub-down the words "With Deepest Sympathy" onto the strip. Using all-purpose glue, add the trip to bottom right-hand corner, as seen in the main photograph.

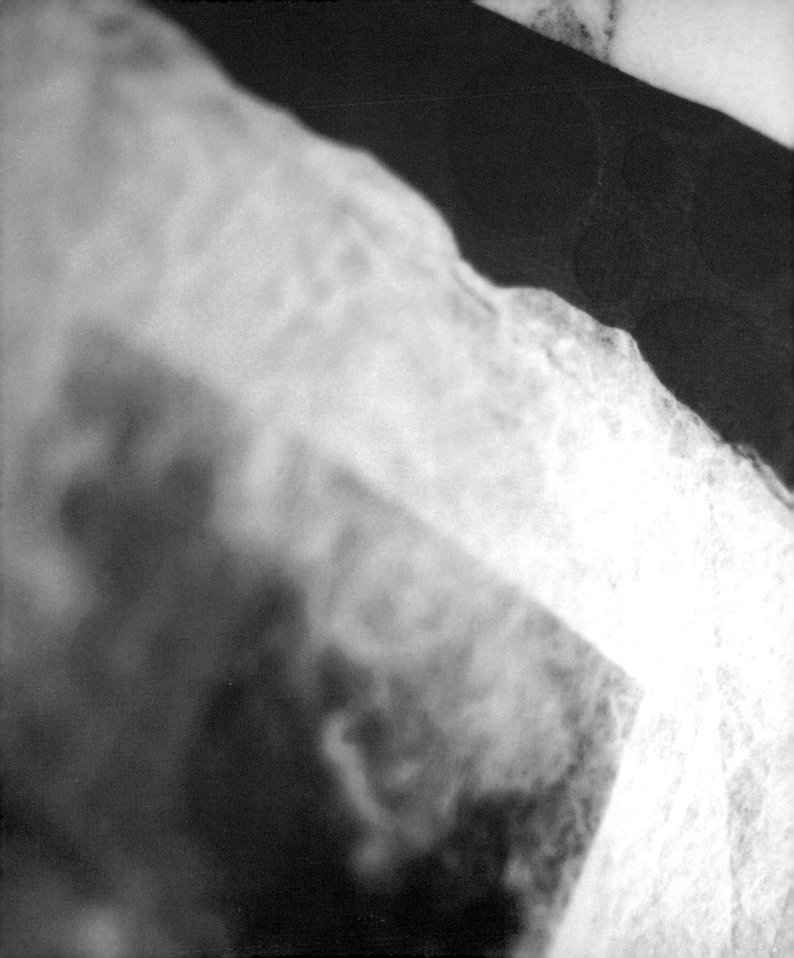

INDEX

INDEX

ACKNOWLEDGMENTS

I would like to extend a huge thank-you to everyone involved in the production of this book. To The BookMaker, Lynn Bryan for asking me to put the knowledge she knew I had into words and pictures, and for guiding me through to the end. Thanks also to Sarah Glennie at G.F. Smith, the paper merchants, for her wonderful paper samples. They make my cards look wonderful. Thanks to Jane Bolsover for her work with me.

As a location to photograph the final cards, I must thank Denise Law of Law & Co. in the quaint, historic village of Stow on the Wold for letting me use her gorgeous shop as a background.

To the publishers, Sterling Publishing Co., Inc., New York, thank you for believing in the concept.

Finally, my biggest thank-you and continued affection goes to my partner, Kevin Harvey, and to my Mum and Dad who tirelessly encourage and enthuse about my ideas. Without their neverending help and support this book would not have been possible.

For more details on my cards and photography, please visit *www.amandahancocks.com*.